CASEBOOKS PUBLISHED AND IN PRINT

Malcolm Lowry

Under the Volcano

A CASEBOOK

EDITED BY

GORDON BOWKER

First published 1987

Published by
MACMILLAN EDUCATION LTD
Houndmills, Basingstoke, Hampshire RG21 2XS
and London
Companies and representatives
throughout the world

Typeset by Wessex Typesetters
(Division of The Eastern Press Ltd)
Frome, Somerset

Printed in Hong Kong

British Library Cataloguing in Publication Data
Malcolm Lowry: Under the volcano: a
selection of critical essays.—(Casebook
series).
1. Lowry, Malcolm. Under the volcano
I. Bowker, Gordon   II. Lowry, Malcolm.
Under the volcano
823'.912   PR6023.096U5
ISBN 0–333–39574–3
ISBN 0–333–39575–1 Pbk

12|95

CONTENTS

6 CONTENTS

System of Titling: here and in the Selection, exterior quotemarks are used for editorially devised captions. In other cases, the caption employs the original title of the writer's book, chapter or section of a book, article or essay (in some instances abbreviated from that), and it is displayed without exterior quotemarks.

GENERAL EDITOR'S PREFACE

The Casebook series, launched in 1968, has become a well-regarded library of critical studies. The central concern of the series remains the 'single-author' volume, but suggestions from the academic community have led to an extension of the original plan, to include occasional volumes on such general themes as literary 'schools' and genres.

Each volume in the central category deals either with one well-known and influential work by an individual author, or with closely related works by one writer. The main section consists of critical readings, mostly modern, collected from books and journals. A selection of reviews and comments by the author's contemporaries is also included, and sometimes comment from the author himself. The Editor's Introduction charts the reputation of the work or works from the first appearance to the present time.

Volumes in the 'general themes' category are variable in structure but follow the basic purpose of the series in presenting an integrated selection of readings, with an Introduction which explores the theme and discusses the literary and critical issues involved.

A single volume can represent no more than a small selection of critical opinions. Some critics are excluded for reasons of space, and it is hoped that readers will pursue the suggestions for further reading in the Select Bibliography. Other contributions are severed from their original context, to which some readers may wish to turn. Indeed, if they take a hint from the critics represented here, they certainly will.

A. E. DYSON

INTRODUCTION

When it was first published, in the United States in 1947, Malcolm Lowry's *Under the Volcano* was greeted as a work of genius and was, for a time, a best-seller. In France, Germany and Italy it was, from the start, regarded as a great modern classic. The critical response in Britain was more muted, and the first edition of 1947 was ultimately remaindered. Not until the book was reprinted there in the 1960s did British scholars and critics begin to give it the recognition it deserved. Anthony Burgess, for example, called it 'a Faustian masterpiece' and rated Lowry 'one of the great dead major novelists',[1] while Muriel Bradbrook has since acclaimed him as 'the greatest novelist (except possibly E. M. Forster) whom Cambridge has produced'.[2] Burgess ascribes the book's early neglect to the climate of provincialism prevailing in Britain in the late 1940s, and Malcolm Bradbury[*] has given the same explanation, adding that writers obsessed with an experimental and cosmopolitan view of art, like Beckett, Durrell and Lowry (all of whom began writing in the 1930s) were driven, by this lack of sympathy, to seek more congenial cultural settings abroad.

Despite his growing reputation, however, Lowry is notably absent from almost every recent survey of the modern British novel. Often he is thought, wrongly, to be American or Canadian – not surprisingly perhaps, since he lived for all but five of his last twenty-three years on the American continent. Yet, although none of his novels and few of his short stories are set in England, and the major influences on his work are foreign, his Englishness is at the very core of his writing.

He was born in New Brighton, Cheshire, in 1909, the youngest son of a Liverpool cotton-broker. He began writing as

[*] Here and elsewhere in the Introduction, an asterisk within square brackets indicates reference to material in the Casebook selection. Numbered references to material or writers cited relate to the Notes for the Introduction, below.

a schoolboy at The Leys School in Cambridge, became hooked on alcohol at fifteen, and went to sea as a deckhand at seventeen. He acquired a passion for jazz while at school and for German Expressionist films as a student in Bonn in 1929. That same year he visited America where the poet Conrad Aiken became his mentor and helped him with the writing of his first novel, *Ultramarine*, which was published in 1933, a year after he graduated from St Catharine's College, Cambridge, with a Third in English. After drifting around the Bohemian fringes of London and Paris, he married an American in 1934 and spent two years in New York before moving with his wife to Mexico. Here he abandoned all other work to concentrate on *Under the Volcano*. In 1938 he went to live in Los Angeles and, when his marriage broke down, moved north to Canada. There he remarried and, from 1940 until 1954, lived in a shack on an inlet just north of Vancouver. After much revision, his Mexican masterpiece was finished at Niagara in 1944. Although he continued to work obsessively on a variety of projects, no further novels were completed and little else was published before his death ('by misadventure') at Ripe in Sussex in June 1957, a month short of his forty-eighth birthday.

Under the Volcano is undoubtedly his greatest achievement, and Lowry came to see it as the centre-piece of his whole fictional *oeuvre* which he planned to organise into an interconnected six-part sequence called 'The Voyage That Never Ends'. This Proustian ambition was never realised, although at his death four novels from the cycle remained at various stages of near-completion. Posthumous publications include a collection of short stories, *Hear Us O Lord from Heaven Thy Dwelling Place* (1961), *Selected Poems* (1962), and his *Selected Letters* (1965). The novella, *Lunar Caustic* (1962) and the longer works, *Dark as the Grave Wherein My Friend Is Laid* (1968) and *October Ferry to Gabriola* (1970), were edited from notes and drafts with the assistance of his widow, Margerie Bonner Lowry, who also edited a collection of stories and memoirs, *Malcolm Lowry: Psalms and Songs*, which appeared in America in 1975. Matthew Corrigan has argued strongly that the publication of edited versions of the unfinished manuscripts was ill-advised and misleading as to the novelist's intentions,[3] and critical opinion has been sharply divided between those

who regard Lowry as a one-novel author and those who
consider his post-*Volcano* fiction a major experimental
achievement anticipating the French *nouveau roman.*[4]

Lowry's progress from the self-conscious pastiche of his early
work to the mastery of *Under the Volcano* was the result of
persistent effort coupled with a distinctly self-critical approach
to his literary art. When he arrived in Mexico with his wife on 2
November (the Day of the Dead) 1936, he was twenty-seven.
Since graduating from Cambridge four years earlier, he had
published only three short stories in addition to *Ultramarine*.
This first novel, which took him five years to complete, is a
highly autobiographical sea-saga about a youthful soul in
torment, based on his experiences as a teenage sailor on a
Liverpool freighter trading to the China Seas. A rather ornate
and derivative work, its interest today lies in the light it throws
on Lowry's apprenticeship as a writer and the elements in it
which foreshadow *Under the Volcano*. The authors who had
excited his passion for the sea as a schoolboy – O'Neill, Conrad,
Melville and Jack London – were supplemented at Cambridge
by Henry James, Faulkner, Yeats, Eliot, Thomas Mann,
Sophocles, Ibsen, Marlowe and Goethe, as well as by the
speculative metaphysical writings of Ouspensky, Charles Fort
and J. W. Dunne (whose theory of serial time left a particularly
strong impression). But the major influences on *Ultramarine*
were the Norwegian, Nordahl Grieg – whose sea novel, *The Ship
Sails On*, he read shortly after arriving in Cambridge – and the
American, Conrad Aiken, from whose novel, *Blue Voyage*, he
borrowed liberally. It was through Aiken that he adopted an
essentially subjective and formalistic theory of the novel, and
was introduced to the techniques of interior monologue and the
use of literary allusions derived from Joyce. Also evident in
Ultramarine are some of the themes, or 'design-governing
postures' as he called them, around which he chose to organise
his array of symbolic references, literary, biographical and
mythological – the themes of Heaven and Hell, the voyage of
self-discovery and of exile and alienation.
    Exile and alienation became more a reality for him after
Cambridge. Alcoholism and anti-social behaviour led him to
break with his family in 1933 and shortly afterwards he broke

with England. In Paris he married Jan Gabrial, a young socialist writer, and, by the end of 1934 they were living in New York where he worked for a year on 'In Ballast to the White Sea', a prodigious novel built around another sea trip, this time to Norway in search of Nordahl Grieg. The manuscript was lost in a house fire in Canada in 1944. This method of seeking experience, sedulously recorded in notes and diaries before being transformed into fictions centred around a thinly disguised Malcolm Lowry, had become his preferred *modus operandi*. In the summer of 1936 he had a brief but particularly searing experience in New York's Bellevue Hospital under treatment for alcoholism, and immediately composed a novella, 'The Last Address', the first version of what became *Lunar Caustic*. This is undoubtedly one of Lowry's finest works and one of the most compelling evocations of mental torment in modern fiction. It also shows considerable technical advance. The suffering of his hero, Bill Plantagenet, is palpably more convincing than that of Dana Hilliot in *Ultramarine*, and the more controlled and powerful prose Lowry had now developed enabled him not only to project the mental anguish of one man, but also to evince a wider landscape of suffering. What Lowry gives us is an apocalyptic vision of an urban wasteland, the lunatic city reflecting the disintegration of modern consciousness. He draws on images from the Expressionist cinema to create a sense of menace and the rhythms of hot jazz to convey the tempo of disconnected speech. Lowry called it 'a masterpiece, or a potential one', and, as Richard Cross rightly observes: 'It clearly points the way to Lowry's Mexican Inferno.'[5]

On his arrival in Mexico all work in progress was set aside so that he could start work on *Under the Volcano*. This began a process of composition which was to last for eight years, during which time the book was written and rewritten in three versions, and some of its chapters redrafted as many as six times. In *Dark as the Grave Wherein My Friend Is Laid*, based on a return visit to Mexico in 1946, the hero, Lowry/Sigbjørn Wilderness, relives the agonies of creating *Under the Volcano* and the long struggle to get it published. He explains the difficulty he had in seeing anything that he wrote as ever finished. 'Anything set down on paper', says Wilderness, 'ceases from that moment progressively to be true – we must consider what happens each morning when the artist is confronted with his work again. Has it not changed in his absence? Of course it has. Even on paper something has happened to it' [pp. 168–9].

Lowry settled in Cuernavaca, a town dominated by the volcano Popocatepetl. Mexico impressed him deeply, its topography and culture taking on a profound significance for him. He found a landscape of great beauty, and a culture which coupled the superstitious death-cult of the native Indians with the avaricious political inheritance of the Conquistadors (a Garden of Eden where Adam is stalked by fearful and malevolent forces). It became, for him, a metaphor of the 1930s and the mirror-image of a visionary mind clouded with self-doubt: the magically-gifted spirit threatened by self-destructive urges. It was, he claimed, 'a good place . . . to set our drama of a man's struggle between the powers of darkness and light. . . . It is paradisal; it is unquestionably infernal.'[6]

Under the Volcano began, he admitted later, as a political parable based on the incident (in ch. 8) of the dying Indian, with his hero representing modern man's inability to cope with the impending threat to his civilisation. In the first draft, he has the French film director, Laruelle, conceiving Geoffrey Firmin, the alcoholic ex-British Consul, as a character in a projected movie. 'Suppose', he says, 'that all the suffering and chaos and conflict of the present were suddenly to take human form. And become conscious of itself! That is the impression I would want to give of my man. . . . If only I could convey the effect of a man who was the very shape and motion of the world's doom.' If it began as a political parable with the Consul as a modern Everyman, over the next eight years it was transformed by stages into so complex and original a work that it defies precise classification, despite the attempts of some early critics to impose one.

The first draft was written fairly rapidly, and by May 1937 he had a complete manuscript to show Conrad Aiken who visited him in Cuernavaca. Douglas Day suggests that it began as a short story, a version of which was published after his death.[7] However, it has been pointed out that in fact this was merely an early draft of ch. 8.[8] Lowry's first wife, Jan, also testifies that it was written as a novel from the start.[9] In September 1937, Jan left him and he departed for Oaxaca, his 'city of dreadful night' where heavy bouts of drinking landed him in jail. Letters he wrote to friends at this time suggest that his sanity was gravely threatened. One of those friends, Arthur Calder-Marshall, believes that this was a deliberate plunge into hell in the hope that eventually a masterpiece would emerge.[10] Lowry left Mexico finally in July 1938.

The Mexican version of the novel was rewritten in the spring of 1940 in Vancouver, where he was living with Margerie Bonner, soon to become his second wife. It was submitted to a New York agent in the following June only to be rejected by thirteen American publishers. In 1941 he began the final revision, completing it on Christmas Eve 1944. A year later he received a copy of an unsympathetic reader's report* from his London publishers, Jonathan Cape. The 'Mexican colour heaped on in shovelfuls' was very well done, it said, but the elaborate flashbacks were 'tedious and unconvincing' and 'the mescal-inspired heebie-jeebies to which Geoffrey has succumbed' were 'too long, wayward and elaborate'.[11] Lowry's reply was a remarkable 15,000 word defence which is also an elegant and ironic commentary on the book and its composition.[12] *Under the Volcano* was accepted simultaneously by Cape and by the American publishers, Reynal and Hitchcock, in April 1946.

In the Preface (completed in 1948) to the French edition of the novel[*], which appeared in 1949, Lowry in turn commented ironically on his letter to Cape. 'The enterprise', he writes, 'was doubtless a foolish one: to give all kinds of good esoteric reasons why the work should stay just as it was in the beginning. Those reasons I have now almost completely forgotten. . . . It is in fact all too true . . . that in all concerning his work a writer assumes the most extraordinary pretensions and is ready to justify anything.' Despite this confession, his letter to Cape has had a profound influence on Lowry criticism, as we shall see.

---

* It is known that the report was by William Plomer (1903–73), novelist, poet and playwright.

The basic structure of the novel had already been established in the 1940 version.[13] Twelve chapters (including the retrospective first chapter from Laruelle's point of view) encompass the last day in the life of Geoffrey Firmin, from the morning after the Red Cross Ball in Quauhnahuac to his being shot and thrown into the *barranca* by fascists in Parián. But in the published version, Yvonne (originally the Consul's English daughter) becomes his returned American wife, and her American boy-friend, Hugh, reappears as his English half-brother. There is a consequent heightening of tension in the dramatic triangle surrounding Yvonne, whose death under the hooves of the runaway horse was also added in the final draft. Day suggests that the more explicit references to the meaning of the symbolism in the earlier draft was Lowry explaining the book to himself and his readers as he went along.[14] And Ronald Binns has shown how, in the published text, the omniscient authorial voice is displaced, literary, political and mythological allusions are rendered more obliquely, and what was earlier represented is given more dramatic expression.[15] This effect was achieved by a radical stylistic transformation which steered the mimetic line further into the consciousness of the characters and away from the material plot.

Binns, here and in a subsequent study[*], explains this change as reflecting a shift in Lowry's political perspective from the late thirties – when he was married to the socialist Jan Gabrial, and was producing socially-aware and economically written fiction – to the early forties, when his wife was the more conservative Margerie Bonner. Under her influence he became interested in the occult, astrology and cabbalism: a curiosity intensified through contact with a disciple of the black magician, Aleister Crowley. All this provided him with layers of allusion which he used to give heightened significance to the Mexican landscape, the Day of the Dead on which the action of the novel takes place, and the drunken hallucinations through which the Consul surveys his guilt-ridden past and agonises over his moral dilemmas with his ghostly familiars. He was also able to use them to give added point to world political events which had taken a more critical and apocalyptic turn by the 1940s. Brian O'Kill's comparison[*] of the two final drafts is a lucid demonstration of how Lowry converted a not untypical

1930s prose style, 'boring, objective and restrained', into the syntactically complex 'churrigueresque' prose of the published version.

Under the Volcano, therefore, bears the traces of both the earlier, socially conscious Lowry striving for 'objectivity', and the later, mystically oriented Lowry lost inside a dark forest of symbols. If Hugh, with his questionable air of conviction, carries the narrative line in the former key, the Consul, with his confused vision, befuddled by alcohol, stumbles along with it in the latter. As a consequence, the book can be read in either mode, one which heightens the political and material landscape of events or one which explores the elaborate symbolic and mental architecture constructed upon it.

This, as we shall see, has given rise to a major division of considered critical responses to the book. Is it best read on the 'immediate' level as a novel of the thirties about the struggle against the dark forces of fascism? Is its true significance, on the other hand, to be found in a 'spatial' reading, exploring the intricate structure of symbols in order to grasp its meaning at a more transcendental and poetic level? Or is it possible to produce a reading which synthesises or orchestrates both modes of the fiction?

Tony Bareham has argued that the finest criticism of the book remains Lowry's own letter to Jonathan Cape.[16] There is, of course, some weight in this, for who better than the author to interpret his own novel? By justifying everything included in terms of its organic integrity and by stressing its poetic and dramatic qualities, Lowry seems to have produced a definitive interpretive blueprint setting out the parameters within which any meaningful criticism must confine itself, and seems also to call for the kind of autonomous reading favoured by New Criticism. And that, as we shall see, is how a number of critics have read the letter since its publication in 1965. Yet Lowry himself seemed aware of that danger, arguing that, though a novel, it could be read in many ways: from a symphony or a poem to a prophesy or a political warning. In characteristic tones of self-mockery, he concludes that 'writers can always grow fancy and learned about their books and say almost

anything at all'; and, though he has emphasised 'the esoteric
element', he 'might have stressed another element just as well'.
No such letter was written to his American publisher, and it
seems that Lowry knew that in England he had to contend with
an uncomprehending and hostile critical establishment, and,
like Eliot, Pound and Joyce before him, was providing a critical
language through which the novel could be understood and
judged. There is also that pointed passage in the Preface (1948)
to the French edition (1949) of *Under the Volcano*[*] in which he
distances himself from his earlier self-justificatory reading by
observing: 'My intention was – and has ever remained to me –
obscure.'

When the novel was published in New York in February
1947, no authorial reading was available, of course.
Nevertheless, it was a considerable critical success. John
Woodburn[*] even emerged uncannily like the ideal reader
Lowry had envisaged in that letter to Cape, reading the book
twice and recognising its 'intricate, convoluted architecture'
while responding to 'its sorrowful music'. It was, Woodburn
claimed 'a work of genius' and Lowry had created his own
genre requiring an entirely new critical language. Robert
Heilman[*] anticipated later, more considered, scholarly
criticism by placing him firmly in the modernist tradition while
acknowledging the novel's moral and political engagement.
'Such a multivalued poetic fiction', he wrote, 'with its sense of
horrifying dissolution, and its submerged, uncertain vision of a
hard new birth off in a clouded time, is apparently the especial
labor of the artistic conscience at our turn of an epoch.' Against
this can be set the few reviews which dismissed the book as
pretentious and derivative, notably that by Jacques Barzun[*]
which provoked a pained letter of protest from Lowry,[17] always
sensitive to charges of plagiarism since accused by Aiken of
borrowing too freely from *Blue Voyage* for *Ultramarine*.

In Britain, one of the warmest receptions came from an
anonymous reviewer in the *Times Literary Supplement*[*] who
considered it a work of 'great imaginative power', its
'passionate interest in the secrets of the fall of man' being akin
to that of Elizabethan tragedy. K. John in the *Illustrated London
News* recognised its contradictions and ambiguities with a
remarkably apt, almost Lowryesque, metaphor – 'You look

down; the bottom is never reached, but the reflections are fascinating.'[18] But these were exceptions and no British critic, writing at this time, joined Woodburn to acclaim the book as 'a work of genius'. Walter Allen[*], while finding it 'a genuinely tragic novel of great concentration and power', complained that 'Mr Lowry's character and method come to us with too many associations clinging to them', and concluded that the impressive quality of the book was marred by a too frequent and conscious use of its literary sources. The *Spectator* dismissed it as prolix and intellectually pretentious.

The favourable shift in British critical opinion came, as we have noted, in the 1960s. In 1962, Philip Toynbee[*] saluted Lowry's gift of natural eloquence and power to shape the language, and echoed John Woodburn's judgement that the book was 'a work of genius' comparable with the best of Hemingway and Scott Fitzgerald. Five years later, writing in the *Spectator*, Anthony Burgess, after a sideswipe at English provincialism, claimed Lowry as one of those writers who saw that 'the novel form's only hope of survival lay in its being taken over by poets', but argued that without the author's own exegesis in the Cape letter, many ordinary readers might fail to recognise the intensity of its conception.[19]

General, comparative studies have located *Under the Volcano* within the tradition of experimental modernism, though Malcolm Bradbury and Richard Cross – and, as we shall see, Stephen Spender – each recognise Lowry as a figure in some ways distinct from it.

Bradbury[*] styles Lowry 'a romantic autodidact' for whom modernism was not central to his work. And, while acknowledging his debt to Joyce, Thomas Wolfe and D. H. Lawrence, he sees the more obvious influence as that of the Romantic poets, 'particularly those associated with voyage and/or suffering', and stresses his literary affiliations with Conrad Aiken and Nordahl Grieg. What renders Lowry's modernistic concern with the 'breakdown of values' different is his individualism: the way he merges the surrounding world with that of his hero through *self*-projection. And yet Bradbury hints that although, like Lowry's *Ultramarine*, *Under the Volcano* is an autobiographical novel, it is a more complicated achievement than that. This is in line with the general critical view that, of all his heroes, the Consul is the one whom Lowry manages most successfully to project outside himself.

Richard Cross[*] also wants to assign Lowry a special place among contemporary modernists, but this time by linking him more closely with Joyce, together with Conrad, Kafka, Mann and Proust – representative of what he calls 'high modernism' as distinct from those, like Nabokov, Borges and Pynchon, who produce a more restricted, *avant-garde*, anti-mimetic, game-playing writing. That does not mean that there is no element of play in Lowry's use of language, no deliberate deployment of puzzling allusions which operate as a deeply ironic commentary on his writing which on occasions approaches self-parody. But Lowry was attempting to say something serious about the human condition as he saw it, and the constant self-mockery, the continual subversion of meaning, the insistent questioning of perception and the confusion of identities in *Under the Volcano*, are employed to prevent himself from collapsing into portentousness and allegory. Gerald Noxon has recorded that, already at Cambridge, Lowry knew what he wanted to say and was searching for new ways to say it. But he was anxious not to abandon the nineteenth-century tradition or to produce a prose which was superficially difficult for the reader.[20]

In his essay of 1965, and so writing earlier than Bradbury, Stephen Spender[*] takes a not dissimilar line. (Although in its entirety a comparative study relevant to Lowry's work as a whole, in our selection we excerpt it so as to let it serve as a pivot between the general discussions of Bradbury and Cross and the studies specific to *Under the Volcano*.) Spender shows how Lowry employs symbolic myth as metaphor and analogy, not as Eliot and Pound do, to transcend the modern condition by identifying its symbolic links with the past, but by taking the symbolism evident in the present to represent the time – the 1930s and 40s. And whereas, with Joyce, 'symbol and myth are used in *Ulysses* in order to absorb the characters at certain moments into a kind of cosmic consciousness . . . Lowry uses them with opposite effect in order to create the interior world of the Consul'. Furthermore, while Stephen Dedalus and Leopold Bloom merge into the cosmos, one is left with the feeling that the Consul *is* the cosmos and that he is also

Malcolm Lowry. For Spender, as for Bradbury, this makes both Lowry and his hero romantics.

Spender also stresses an aspect which puts the 'modernist' interpretation in a non-literary perspective: that of the film camera. '. . . the most direct influence on this extraordinary book is not, I would suggest, from other novelists, but from films, most of all perhaps those of Eisenstein. The movies – that is, the old, silent, caption-accompanied movies – are felt throughout the novel.'

While there has been some degree of critical consensus about locating Lowry within the modernist tradition, there has been none over the best method of reading him. Much of the early criticism tended to stress the poetic and literary qualities of *Under the Volcano*. David Markson, Lowry's disciple, for example, tried, by tracing sources, to demonstrate a symbolic patterning borrowed from Homer, similar to that in Joyce's *Ulysses*.[21] Victor Doyen[*], writing in the aftermath of the publication of Lowry's letter to Cape, approaches the novel as poem, taking his lead from Joseph Frank's essay, 'Spatial Form in Modern Literature'.[22] An advocate of New Criticism, Frank argued that the work of modernists like Joyce, Eliot and Pound were required to be read 'spatially' – that is, apprehended in a moment rather than as a sequence. The work of the critic is therefore to disclose and grasp as a unity patterns of meaning scattered in references throughout a work.

This approach does seem to be invited by Lowry's letter to Cape, which concentrates on the poetic, though he does warn that there are other ways of reading the book. The result is a catalogue of images and symbols which are meant to unlock the meaning of the book for the passive reader, and Lowry's art is portrayed as 'static'.[23] Other 'spatial' readings which have attempted to confine the book to a single meaning are Perle Epstein's cabbalistic interpretation, Kilgallin's attempt to argue that the Faustian theme provides its central design, and, even more tenuously, Barnes's assigning this role to the myth of Sisyphus.[24] The linear base of the narrative seems thereby to be denied, and its social, biographical and historical contexts excluded as irrelevant.

Dale Edmonds[*], by contrast, emphasises the mimetic or 'immediate' level as the one on which 'the novel communicates most effectively'. While stressing that this is not the only way to read it, he argues that it is essential to all other readings. He picks out five major aspects of the story: (1) the Weight of the Past; (2) Salvage Operations directed towards the Consul; (3) the Mosaic of Doom – Firmin's involvement with anti-fascist elements; (4) the Consul's alcoholism and its possible causes; (5) the theme of the necessity of love (*No se peude vivir sin amar* – 'one cannot live without loving').

In dealing with the Consul's involvement with anti-fascism, Edmonds makes the case, based on a variety of clues in the story, that Geoffrey Firmin is engaged in spying and that his murder is the logical outcome of his being exposed. It is clear from Lowry's letter that he planted this suspicion deliberately but wanted it left at no more than that. There are here, however, fictions within fictions, like the boxes within boxes which the layout of El Farolito, the cantina where Geoffrey meets his end, suggests. The fictional world of the Consul is a labyrinth riddled with mystery, strewn with false clues leading to false trails; it is a dark wood in which he is lost, passing from a clouded past into an obscure, uncertain and threatening future. Expectations are subverted by a ruptured narrative line; the truth is asserted and immediately questioned, hopes raised then dashed. Although Edmonds supplies valuable background information on the Mexican political context of the late 1930s, he risks, by linking it too closely to the Consul's action and his fate, imposing a closed reading on the narrative line similar to the way Doyen attempts to place one on the symbolic structure.

However, Edmonds does demonstrate that there *is* a definable plot, and Andrew Pottinger[*] extends the analysis of the 'immediate level' to an examination of ch. 12 of *Under the Volcano*, demonstrating how, between versions, Lowry made the story line more ambiguous. He shows how moral sanction is removed from the narrative voice, introducing uncertainty into the Consul's point of view, and giving the book 'a dimension of irony, centred on the theme of alienation'. This enables him to explain Firmin's death at the hands of the Chief of Rostrums. Alienated characters fail to communicate; the murder is a misunderstanding, not unlike Meursault's murder of the Arab in Camus's *L'Étranger*.

A reading at the 'immediate' level can open out the text from the enclosure superimposed by 'spatial' readings, but also it can, in turn, lead us to ignore the figurative interplay between narrative line and symbolic reference. One proposed synthesis is Day's *Gestalt* interpretation which encompasses five thematic levels in the work: the *chthonic*, or earthbound; the human; the political; the magical; and the religious.[25] Day offers no indication of how these levels are interrelated, and so the *Gestalt* reading fails to avoid the inertia of earlier 'static' analyses.

Wood[*] suggests one approach which promises to overcome this difficulty by applying to *Under the Volcano* Northrop Frye's theory of literary genres. He echoes some of the early reviewers by arguing that the book cannot easily be classified. However, he does not, like John Woodburn, claim that Lowry has created an entirely new genre, but rather that it contains elements of all four described by Frye – novel, confession, anatomy and romance. It is, Wood argues, a *novel* in the great English tradition, *confessional* in form in the mode of a *romantic* quest which is, at the same time, an *anatomy* of death. These generic elements of the book are to be seen in different kinds of contrapuntal movement between the narrative line and the mythic patterning of the book.

A more elaborate attempt at synthesis is presented by Sherrill Grace[*] who, like O'Kill and Pottinger, examines the transition from the penultimate to the published version, especially evident in Lowry's use of J. W. Dunne's theory of serial time, made explicit in the former but absorbed at a deeper level in the latter. She stresses 'the principle of containment' which is the novel's trochal, wheel-like form. This circular configuration plus a reflexive movement, she argues, overshadows and subsumes the sequential narrative of events. Grace therefore, while recognising the 'immediate' level of the text, stresses in the end its 'spatial form'. It is by interrupting the temporal narrative flow and freezing time, and thereby giving us 'a heightened awareness of space', that Lowry is able to evoke a sense of timelessness. By 'compacting' time, Lowry is able to present past, present and future together as indistinguishable, and so produce an 'intense sensation of simultaneity' which perfectly projects 'the state of Geoffrey's soul'. Her reading is cast, then, in terms of the play of rhetorical figures, using Jakobson's distinction between metaphor and

metonymy: a structuralist reading which reduces the book's
meaning to the key 'secret passage' in Lowry's *magnum mysterium*
– not more nor less than an archetypal metaphysical concept of
consciousness and physical expansion.

The problem with this approach, as Christopher Norris has
pointed out,[26] is that a structuralist reading boils down
ultimately to a gloss on New Criticism. The static wheel image
is too much like the intricate web of symbols in Doyen, and
ignores Lowry's own failure to specify any single meaning in his
Cape letter, or that one kind of reading precludes another or
works against it. A political reading, such as Edmonds
provides, strains against Grace's structural reduction to a
metaphysics of space and time, as hers does against his. One
might well present an analysis that emphasises conflicting
voices in the text as one that identifies the smooth articulation
of levels or figures.

It is this element of conflict which is stressed by Ronald
Binns[*]. He picks out, for example, 'the conflicting lives and
values of the four *angst*-ridden expatriates' (the book's main
characters), its 'disjunctive modernist style and turbulent plot',
'the obscure, fractured and second-hand nature of the Consul's
knowledge', and the 'uncertainty, hesitation, ignorance and
doubt' which 'are the basic conditions of Lowry's fictional
world'. He seems to agree with Grace in arguing that 'the
structure of the novel endorses the Consul's belief in historical
cycles'; but against that, he points out, is posed 'Hugh's linear
materialistic philosophy'. He also notes that there are in the
text other voices and visions beside those of the Consul (upon
which Grace focuses). There are, for example, the critical voice
and vision of Hugh and the off-stage Juan Cerillo articulating
an alternative view of Mexico and the world. It is this, says
Binns, which subjects the 'solipsism embodied most
profoundly by the Consul' to 'attack and critical irony'. And,
although the critical voice which threatens the Consul's
'inward-looking values' is more displaced in the published
version, and omitted completely in the later novels,
nevertheless, in *Under the Volcano*, Lowry does exhibit 'the
historian's willingness to see the drama of both sides'. One
might add, of course, that there are other voices to be heard,
such as Laruelle's and Yvonne's, as well as those of minor
characters, such as the fascists.

There is, then, a wide range of disagreement among critics, except about the stature of *Under the Volcano*. Presumably those who do not rate it highly do not write about it. That it is a novel in the modernist tradition, apocalyptic, symbolist and experimental, is not in dispute. That it is a novel that bears a single reading seems no longer a fashionable idea, though whether it is a novel of 'form' or to do with social, political and historical ideas, is still a running issue. The stress is still, apparently, either on harmony and synthesis or upon conflict and disruption. Parallels can be found in critical responses to similarly encyclopedic works, such as *Moby Dick*, *Ulysses* and *Gravity's Rainbow*, and it may be the fate of such novels to be read by each generation in its own way, reflecting the prevailing state of critical ferment.

Under the Volcano is a perplexing, contradictory, uncertain novel of great imaginative power set in a nightmarish, ghost-ridden landscape of allegorical proportions. But it is also set in a precise historical context in which matters of life and death are being decided. And although it is about the self-destructive urge in modern man, it is also a celebration of life. It is worth remembering that Lowry conceived of his Mexican Hell's giving way eventually to a Northern Paradise. Geoffrey Firmin is ejected from the Paradise Garden into the abyss, as the final epigraph reminds us; but returning to the beginning of the book, as Lowry instructs us to do, we find the quotation from Goethe: 'Whosoever unceasingly strives upward . . . him can we save.' Lowry also intended it to be a funny book, and was most upset that few critics regarded it as such. One thing is certain; the critical debate about *Under the Volcano* will continue, and perhaps in the very complex manner the reader is invited to respond to it lies its greatest value.

NOTES

1. Anthony Burgess, 'Europe's Day of the Dead', *Spectator* (20 Jan. 1967), p. 74.

2. Muriel Bradbrook, *Malcolm Lowry: His Art and Early Life* (London, 1974), p. 1.

3. Matthew Corrigan, 'Malcolm Lowry, New York Publishing, and the "New Illiteracy"', *Encounter*, 35 (July 1970), pp. 82–93.

4. Douglas Day, *Malcolm Lowry: A Biography* (New York, 1973; London, 1974), takes the former view; the latter is held by Muriel Bradbrook, op. cit.

5. Richard K. Cross, *Malcolm Lowry: A Preface to His Fiction* (Chicago, 1980; London, 1980), p. 24.

6. *Selected Letters of Malcolm Lowry*, edited by Harvey Breit and Margerie Bonner Lowry (1965; Harmondsworth, 1985), p. 67.

7. Ibid., p. 216. See also Malcolm Lowry, 'Under the Volcano', *Prairie Schooner*, 37 (Winter 1963–64), pp. 284–300 (posthumous publication).

8. Brian O'Kill, 'Malcolm Lowry', *Times Literary Supplement* (26 April 1964), p. 447.

9. Gordon Bowker (ed.), *Malcolm Lowry Remembered* (London, 1985), p. 120.

10. Ibid., p. 113.   11. Day, op cit., pp. 316–17 (Plomer's report).

12. H. Breit and M. Bonner (eds), *Selected Letters of Malcolm Lowry* (1965; Harmondsworth, 1985), pp. 57–88.

13. Day, op. cit., pp. 258–68.   14. Ibid., p. 264.

15. Ronald Binns, 'Self-Consciousness and Form in the Fiction of Malcolm Lowry', unpublished Ph. D. thesis (University of East Anglia, 1976), p. 85.

16. T. Bareham, 'Paradigms of Hell: Symbolic Patterning in *Under the Volcano*', in B. S. Benedikz (ed.), *On the Novel* (London, 1971), p. 114.

17. *Selected Letters*, p. 143.

18. K. John, 'Fiction of the Week', *Illustrated London News* (17 Sept. 1947), p. 356.

19. Burgess, op. cit., p. 74.

20. Gerald Noxon, 'Malcolm Lowry 1930', in ibid., p. 51.

21. David Markson, 'Myth in *Under the Volcano*, *Prairie Schooner*, 37 (Winter 1963–64), pp. 339–46.

22. Joseph Frank, 'Spatial Forms in Modern Literature', in M. Schorer, J. Miles and G. McKenzie (eds), *Criticism: The Foundations of Modern Literary Judgement* (New York, 1948), pp. 379–92.

23. See Terence Wright, '*Under the Volcano*: The Static Art of Malcolm Lowry', *Ariel*, I, no. 4 (Oct: 1970), pp. 67–76.

24. See: Perle Epstein, *The Private Labyrinth of Malcolm Lowry* (New York, 1969); Anthony R. Kilgallin, 'Faust and *Under the Volcano*', *Canadian Literature*, 26 (Autumn 1965), pp. 43–54; and Jim Barnes, 'The Myth of Sisyphus in *Under the Volcano*', *Prairie Schooner*, 42 (Winter 1969), pp. 341–8.

25. Day, op. cit., pp. 326–50.

26. Christopher Norris, *Deconstruction: Theory and Practice* (London, 1982), p. 8.

Editor's Note on Pagination

The latest Penguin edition (1985) of *Under the Volcano* has caused some confusion because it includes, for the first time in its issuing of the novel, Lowry's letter to Cape. In adding 40 pages, in consecutive arabic-numbering with the novel's text, the new edition's inclusion of the letter radically alters the pagination of the novel. (It is regrettable that a distinct system of pagination for the letter was not employed.) Consequently several studies on Lowry which cite the Penguin edition of 1962 now have page-numbers at odds with the 1985 version (e.g., ch. 1 of the 1962 version began on page 9; in the 1985 version, it begins on p. 49).

In our selection we seek – where the context requires it – to clarify the pagination problem in material citing the Penguin edition by giving in parenthesis the new pagination after references to the earlier version of 1962 – e.g., p. 9(49).

PART ONE

The Art of
Malcolm Lowry

Malcolm Lowry Preface to a Novel (1948)

[*Editorial Note*: Lowry wrote this in 1948 for the French edition of *Under the Volcano* (published in Paris in 1949) when collaborating with its translator, Clarisse Francillon. According to George Woodcock, the final version of the Preface was prepared in French from Lowry's English notes, so that no English original of it exists. The version given here is that translated by Woodcock from the French version.]

I like Prefaces. I read them. Sometimes I do not read farther, and it is possible that you may do the same. In that case, this preface will have failed in its purpose, which is to make your access to my book a little more easy. Above all, reader, do not regard these pages as an affront to your intelligence. They prove rather that the author here and there questions his own.

To begin with, his very style may assume an embarrassing resemblance to that of the German writer Schopenhauer describes, who wished to express six things at the same time instead of discussing them one after the other. 'In those long, rich parenthetical periods, like boxes enclosing boxes, and crammed more full than roast geese stuffed with apples, one's memory above all is put to the task, when understanding and judgement should have been called upon to do their work.'

But to take a criticism of style – as Schopenhauer conceived it – as a criticism of the mind and character of the author or even, as others would like, of the man himself, is beside the point. That at least is what I wrote in 1946, on board a bauxite ship in the middle of the waves between New Orleans and Port-au-Prince. That preface was never published. As for this one, the first reason for my drafting it was the fact that in 1945 my book received a very lukewarm welcome from an English firm (which has since done me the honour of publishing it). Although the publishers considered the work 'important and honest', they suggested wide corrections which I was reluctant to make. (You would have reacted in the same way had you written a book and been so tormented by it that you rejected

and rewrote it many times.) Among other things, I was advised
to suppress two or three characters, to reduce the twelve
chapters to six, to change the subject, which was too similar to
that of *Poison*; in short, to throw my book out of the window and
write another. Since now I have the honour of being translated
into French, I take up once again my letter of reply to my
publisher and friend in London. The enterprise was doubtless a
foolish one: to give all kinds of good esoteric reasons why the
work should stay just as it was in the beginning.

Those reasons I have now almost completely forgotten, and
perhaps that is lucky for you. It is in fact all too true, as
Sherwood Anderson has remarked, that in all concerning his
work a writer assumes the most extraordinary pretensions and
is ready to justify anything. It is also likely that one of the few
honest remarks an author has ever made was that of Julien
Green on the subject, I believe, of his masterly *Minuit*: 'My
intention was – and has ever since remained to me – obscure.'

In writing this book, which was started when I was
twenty-six (I am now about to salute my fortieth year) and
finished five years ago, my intention did not at first seem to me
obscure, although it became more so as the years went on. But,
whether obscure or not, it still remains a fact that one of my
intentions was to write a book.

And, indeed, my intention was not to write a tedious book. I
do not believe a single author, even the most irascible of them
all, has ever had the deliberate intention of wearying his reader,
though it has been said that boredom can be used as a
technique. But once this book did in fact appear boring to a
reader – and a professional reader at that – I thought it
necessary to reply to the observations of that professional
reader,* and here is the gist of what I wrote. All this may
perhaps appear to you terribly vain and pompous, but how can
you explain to someone who claims to have been bored by your
prose that he was in the wrong for letting himself be bored?

* [Ed.] The reader's report from Cape which so upset Lowry, and led to his
writing a lengthy reply (he estimated it at 20,000 words, but 15,000 is more
precise), was revealed by Michael Howard, in his *History of Jonathan Cape*
(1972), to have been William Plomer, the poet, novelist and critic. The report
was to have appeared among Lowry's *Selected Letters*, but was removed by the
editors after strenuous objections from Plomer.

'Dear Sir', I wrote then, 'Thank you for your letter of the 29th November 1945. I received it only on New Year's Eve. Moreover, it reached me here in Mexico where, entirely by chance, I am living in the tower which served as a model for the house of one of my characters. Ten years ago I had only seen that tower from the outside, and – in chapter vi – it became the place where my hero too experienced some slight vexations as a result of delayed mail. . . .'*

Then I went on to say that if my work had already assumed the classic form of the printed page instead of the sad and desolate aspect which characterises an unpublished manuscript, the opinion of the reader would certainly have been entirely different because of the various critical judgements that would have assailed his ears. Since the tiresomeness or otherwise of the beginning of *Under the Volcano* appeared to me dependent on the reader's state of mind, on his readiness to seize the author's intention, I suggested – doubtless in desperation of my cause – that a brief preface might neutralise the reactions which my professional reader foresaw. I continued thus: 'If you tell me that a good wine needs no label, I may perhaps reply that I am not talking about wine but about mescal, and that even more than a label – once one has crossed the threshold of the tavern – mescal calls for the accompaniment of both salt and lemon. I hope at least that such a preface may bring a little lemon and salt.'

In this way I wrote a letter of round about 20,000 words, which took me the time I might just as well have employed on starting the first draft of a new novel, even more boring than the other. And since, in the eyes of my reader, the first chapter seemed to be the novel's greatest crime, I limited myself to an analysis of that long first chapter which establishes the themes and counter-themes of the book, which sets the tone, which harmonises the symbolism.

The narrative, I explained, begins on All Souls' Day, in November, 1939, in a hotel called Casino de la Selva – selva

---

* [Ed.] We retain here Lowry's use of roman numerals for chapters, but elsewhere in the Casebook – to standardise varying usages among the many contributers – arabic numerals are employed. All of Lowry's chapter references here relate to the same chapters in the published work; its structure was not altered after submission.

meaning *wood*. And perhaps it would not be out of place to mention here that the book was first of all conceived rather pretentiously on the sempiternal model of Gogol's *Dead Souls*, and as the first leaf of the triptych of a kind of drunken *Divine Comedy*. *Purgatory* and *Paradise* were to follow, with the protagonist, like Chichikov, becoming at each stage slightly better or worse, according to one's point of view. (However, if one is to believe a recent authority, the incredible Vladimir Nabokov, the progression postulated by Gogol was rather: Crime, Punishment, Redemption; Gogol threw almost all of Punishment and Redemption into the fire.) The theme of the dark wood, introduced once again in chapter vii when the Consul enters a lugubrious cantina called El Bosque, which also means *wood*, is resolved in chapter ix, which relates the death of the heroine and in which the wood becomes reality and also fatality.

This first chapter is shown through the eyes of a French film producer, Jacques Laruelle. He establishes a kind of survey of the terrain, just as he expresses the slow, melancholy and tragic rhythm of Mexico itself: Mexico, the meeting place of many races, the ancient battleground of social and political conflicts where, as Waldo Frank, I believe, has shown, a colourful and talented people maintained a religion which was virtually a cult of death. It is the ideal setting for the struggle of a human being against the powers of darkness and light.

After leaving the Casino de la Selva, Jacques Laurelle finds himself looking into the barranca which plays a great part in the story, and which is also the ravine, that cursed abyss which in our age every man presents to himself, and also, more simply, if the reader prefers it, the sewer.

The chapter ends in another cantina where people are taking refuge during an unseasonal storm, while elsewhere, all over the world, people are crawling into the air-raid shelters; then the lights go out, just as, all over the world as well, they are going out. Outside, in that night created by the tempest, the luminous wheel is turning.

That wheel is the Ferris wheel erected in the middle of the square, but it is also, if you like, many other things: the wheel of the law, the wheel of Buddha. It is even eternity, the symbol of the Everlasting Return. That wheel, which demonstrates the very form of the book, can also be considered in a cinematographic manner as the wheel of Time, which is about to turn in an inverse direction, until we reach the preceding year. For the beginning of the second chapter brings us to All Souls' Day a year before, in November 1938.

At this point I tried modestly to insinuate that my little book seemed to me denser and deeper, composed and carried out with more care than the English publisher supposed; that if its meanings had escaped the reader, or if the latter had deemed uninteresting the meanings that float on the surface of the narrative, this might have been due at least in part to a merit rather than a failing of mine. In fact, had not the more accessible aspect of the book been designed so carefully that the reader did not wish to take the trouble of pausing to go below the surface? 'If that is true', I added, not without a certain vanity, 'for how many books can it be said?'

In a more sentimental tone, but with only an appearance of greater modesty, I then wrote as follows: 'Since I am asking for a re-reading of the *Volcano*, in the light of certain aspects which may not have occurred to you, and since I do not wish to undertake a defence of every paragraph, it may be as well for me to admit that in my view the principal failing of the book, from which all the others flow, lies in something which cannot be remedied; the mental baggage of the book is subjective rather than objective; it would better suit a poet – I do not say a good poet – than a novelist, and it is a baggage very difficult to carry as far as its destination. On the other hand, just as a tailor who knows his customer's deformity tries to hide it, I have tried as far as possible to hide the faults of my understanding. But since the conception of the work was primarily poetic, these deformities may hardly matter after all. Besides, poems often call for several readings before their meaning is revealed – is exposed in the mind as I believe Hopkins said – and it is precisely that notion which you have overlooked.'

I demanded the most serious examination of the text, and I asked how, without appreciating its contents, the reader had reached his view that the book was too long, particularly since his reaction might well be different after a second reading. Did not readers, just as much as authors, take a risk of falling over

themselves by going too fast? And what a boring book it must
be if so hasty a reading were all that could be granted!

I went on to explain that my novel consists of twelve
chapters, and the main part of the narrative is contained within
a single day of twelve hours. In the same way, there are twelve
months in a year and the whole book is enclosed within the
limits of a year, while that deeper layer of the novel – or the
poem – which derives from myth is linked at this point with the
Jewish Cabbala, where the number twelve is of the greatest
importance. The Cabbala is used for poetic ends because it
represents Man's spiritual aspirations. The Tree of Life, its
emblem, is a kind of complicated ladder whose summit is called
Kether, or Light, while somewhere in its midst an abyss opens
out. The spiritual domain of the Consul is probably Qliphoth,
the world of husks and demons, represented by the Tree of Life
turned upside down and governed by Beelzebub, the God of
Flies. All this was not essential for the understanding of the
book; I mentioned it in passing so as to give the feeling, as
Henry James has said, 'that depths exist'.

In the Jewish Cabbala the abuse of magic powers is
compared to drunkenness or the abuse of wine, and is
expressed, if I remember rightly, by the Hebrew word *sod*.
Another attribution of the word *sod* signifies garden, or
neglected garden, and the Cabbala itself is sometimes
considered a garden (naturally similar to that where grew the
tree of forbidden fruit which gave us the Knowledge of Good
and Evil), with the Tree of Life planted in the middle. In one
way or another these matters are at the base of many of our
legends regarding the origins of man, and William James, if not
Freud, might be in agreement with me when I affirm that the
agonies of the drunkard find a very close parallel in the agonies
of the mystic who has abused his powers. Here the Consul has
brought everything together in a magnificently drunken
fashion. In Mexico, mescal is a formidable drink but a drink
which one can get in any cantina much more easily, if I may say
so, than Scotch whisky in the Impasse des Deux-Anges. (Let
me say in passing that I see I have done wrong to mescal and
tequila, which are drinks I like very much, and for that I should
perhaps present my apologies to the Mexican government.)
But mescal is also a drug which is taken in the form of mescalin,

and the transcendance of its effects is one of the best-known experiments among occultists. It seems as though the Consul has confused the two states, and perhaps after all he is not in the wrong.

This novel, to use a phrase of Edmund Wilson, has for its subject the forces that dwell within man and lead him to look upon himself with terror. Its subject is also the fall of man, his remorse, his incessant struggle towards the light under the weight of the past, which is his destiny. The allegory is that of the Garden of Eden, the garden representing the world from which we are now even a little more under the threat of ejection than at the moment when I wrote this book. On one level, the drunkenness of the Consul may be regarded as symbolising the universal drunkenness of war, of the period that precedes war, no matter when. Throughout the twelve chapters, the destiny of my hero can be considered in its relationship to the destiny of humanity.

'I hold to the number twelve', I then added. 'It is as if I heard a clock sounding midnight for Faust, and when I think of the slow progression of the chapters, I feel that neither more nor less than twelve should satisfy me. For the rest, the book is stratified in numerous planes. My effort has been to clarify as far as possible whatever at first presented itself to me in a complicated and esoteric manner. The novel can be read simply as a novel during which you may – if you wish – skip whole passages, but from which you will get far more if you skip nothing at all. It can be regarded as a kind of symphony or opera, or even as something like a cowboy film. I wanted to make of it a jam session, a poem, a song, a tragedy, a comedy, a farce. It is superficial, profound, entertaining, boring, according to one's taste. It is a prophecy, a political warning, a cryptogram, a crazy film, an absurdity, a writing on the wall. It can be thought of as a kind of machine; it works, you may be sure, for I have discovered that to my own expense. And in case you should think that I have made of it everything except a novel, I shall answer that in the last resort it is a real novel that I have intended to write, and even a damnably serious novel.'

In short, I made terrific efforts to explain my own ideas of this unfortunate volume; I waged a notable battle for the work as it stood, as it was finally printed, and as it today appears for my French readers. And remember, I wrote all that in Mexico, in the very place where ten years before I had started my book, and in the end I received, from the hands of the same tiny postman who brought the Consul his delayed postcard, the news that it had been accepted.

After this long preamble, my dear French reader, it would perhaps be honest of me to admit to you that the idea I cherished in my heart was to create a pioneer work in its own class, and to write at last an authentic drunkard's story. I do not know whether I have succeeded. And now, friend, I beg you continue your walk along the Seine, and please replace this book where you found it, in the second-hand bookseller's 100-franc box.

MALCOLM LOWRY
September 1948

Brian O'Kill   Aspects of Language in *Under the Volcano*   (1978)

'If Mr Lowry would sieve out his style a bit, and prune the abandoned, brilliant image, I think he would be . . . an outstanding writer.'[1] So wrote one of the original reviewers of *Under the Volcano* in 1947, and an easy scornful reply is not justified merely by hindsight and Lowry's fairly steady reputation. Since recent studies of his work continue to hint at some uneasiness about his use of language, we are still faced with the implication that the language of *Under the Volcano* is an optional decorative element which could be sieved, pruned or otherwise altered without shaking the work's foundations. That is, I think, a fallacious reason for a valid line of inquiry; for better or worse, Lowry's characteristic methods of verbal organisation are very closely related to the total construction and coherence of the novel.

Lowry was only too ready to anticipate adverse judgments on almost every point of his immensely laboured and self-conscious novel, and in his anxiously jocular preface to a

French edition he pretended to admit that his style bore 'an embarrassing resemblance to that of the German writer Schopenhauer describes, who wished to express six things at the same time instead of discussing them one after the other. "In those long, rich parenthetical periods, like boxes enclosing boxes, and crammed more full than roast geese stuffed with apples, one's memory above all is put to the task, when understanding and judgment should have been called upon to do their work." '[2] Within *Under the Volcano* one can find comparable phrases providing, according to the author, 'a suggestion that the book was satirizing itself'.[3] Thus, within a Mexican tourist-guide which offers an ironic perversion of the English language, there are references to 'a churrigueresque [overloaded] style', 'overloaded art work', 'an overloading style', 'an overloaded and embellished style'.[4] Another revealing image of Lowry's attitude to his work is suggested by his protagonist's reaction to an overgrown garden: 'Oddly enough, it did not strike him as being nearly so "ruined" as it had earlier appeared. Such chaos as might exist even lent an added charm. He liked the exuberance of the unclipped growth at hand' [p. 131(171)]*

The 'unclipped growth' and the attempt to 'express six things at the same time' are concomitant features of the novel which largely account for its language and form. As an initial specimen of Lowry's method, here is a fairly typical sentence from the opening chapter: Jacques Laruelle, a French ex-film-director, walks (in a circle, as Lowry's characters usually move and think) around the Mexican town of Quauhnahuac, ruminating upon, among other things, his desire for the deceased wife of his deceased friend Geoffrey Firmin:

His passion for Yvonne (whether or not she'd ever been much good as an actress was beside the point, he'd told her the truth when he said she would have been more than good in any film he made) had brought back to his heart, in a way he could not have explained, the first time that alone, walking over the meadows from Saint Près, the sleepy French village of backwaters and locks and grey disused watermills where he was lodging, he had seen, rising slowly and wonderfully and with boundless beauty above the stubble fields

---

* For variant pagination in citations from Penguin editions, see 'Editors Note on Pagination' after the Introduction, above.

blowing with wildflowers, slowly rising into the sunlight, as centuries before
the pilgrims straying over those same fields had watched them rise, the twin
spires of Chartres Cathedral.   [p. 18(58)]

The most marked and characteristic feature of this sentence
is the use of self-embedding clauses interrupting the main
syntactical movement. The basic statement is split into five
isolated sections: 'His passion for Yvonne / had brought back
to his heart / the first time that alone / he had seen / the twin
spires of Chartres Cathedral.' Between each unit and its
successor there is at least one intervening modification: a
parenthetical disjunct, participle clauses premodifying subject
and object, an appositive noun-phrase, and adverbial, relative
and comparative clauses. Thus four-fifths of the sentence, 100
words out of 124, consists of grammatically peripheral
material, of elaborations and qualifications inserted into the
framework at almost every possible point.

These frequent interruptions have an effect, on one level, of
mimicking the hesitations and divagations of spontaneous
mental activity; but there are also larger authorial intentions at
stake. Lowry seems to avoid, for as long as possible, finishing
and defining the sentence as a unit: through the withholding of
the grammatical resolution until the very end of the sentence,
all the elements are kept in fluid suspension until the last; the
middle of the sentence is held together not by strong syntactical
organisation but by the non-committal verbal repetition of
'rising slowly . . . slowly rising . . . rise'. Such a suspension and
recapitulation of syntax, necessitating repetition of a key word
after a number of modifiers have disrupted the basic structure,
is not an uncommon feature in Lowry's work. Peripheral
material often seems to acquire so much weight and
momentum of its own that it threatens to destroy the shape and
coherence of a sentence – just as, on first or on tenth reading,
the main structures of the novel may seem to be obscured by so
much material of little apparent relevance.

On closer examination, however, the main digression in this
sentence is seen to make a fairly important contribution. No
doubt it is a manifestation of Lowry's restless habit of sticking
every possible fragment of his experience into his work,
however tangential it may seem to his immediate purposes; it

must have been in 1933 or 1934 that he himself first visited Chartres, and ten years later he suddenly inserted the material into the middle of a description of Mexican landscape. But the digression is probably not irrelevant to his broader intentions. The opening paragraph of *Under the Volcano*, symbolically locating Quauhnahuac at the heart of the world, signals clearly enough that he is attempting to write not just about a few mediocre people in a particular locality at a specific period of history, but also about universal human history and consciousness. If the characters of the novel are presented as symptomatic of universal processes, it is also true that universality exists within them. It is quite characteristic that, within a sentence describing the thoughts of a modern man in Mexico, the reader is given a brief picture of medieval pilgrims, offering a glimpse of another time, another place, almost of another world. Within Lowry's ramifications, Mexico can be transformed into 'every sort of landscape at once' [p. 15(55)]; within the inclusive consciousness created in the novel, all kinds of disparate facts and feelings can be piled together, briefly illuminated by juxtaposition if not by any defined relationship. Syntactical digression and expansion might therefore be seen as one of the chief devices by which Lowry tries to merge specific and universal references.

As a further example, here is a sentence from the opening pages of the second chapter, narrating the moment of Yvonne Firmin's return to the town in which she left her husband a year previously:

Ashamed, numb with nostalgia and anxiety, reluctant to enter the crowded bar, though equally reluctant to have the taxidriver go in for her, Yvonne, her consciousness so lashed by wind and air and voyage she still seemed to be travelling, still sailing into Acapulco harbour yesterday evening through a hurricane of immense and gorgeous butterflies swooping seaward to greet the *Pennsylvania* – at first it was as though fountains of multicoloured stationery were being swept out of the saloon lounge – glanced defensively round the square, really tranquil in the midst of this commotion, of the butterflies still zigzagging overhead or past the heavy open ports, endlessly vanishing astern, *their* square, motionless and brilliant in the seven o'clock morning sunlight, silent yet somehow poised, expectant, with one eye half open already, the merry-go-rounds, the Ferris wheel, lightly dreaming, looking forward to the fiesta later – the ranged rugged taxis too that were looking forward to something else, a taxi strike that afternoon, she'd been confidentially informed.   [pp. 48–9(88–9)]

When Albert Erskine, editor for Lowry's American publishers, objected that this sentence was 'pretty difficult to come to grips with simply on account of its syntax and might be more effective if clarified', the author was quick to insist that 'the overlapping style at this point is necessary'.[5] At least Lowry did not seek to abrogate his authorial responsibility by claiming here that this is 'Yvonne's style', a variety of language dictated by the character at the centre of the experience. These verbal torrents are not confined to Yvonne, and it would be easy to exaggerate the effect of the novel's shifting viewpoint upon its language. Although most of the novel is ostensibly mediated through the minds of its characters – each chapter through the consciousness of one of the four chief personages, whose viewpoint is explicitly established at the outset – this device is not maintained with inflexible consistency and is not a rigorously determining influence upon the novel's narrative and stylistic system. It was not established at all until a fairly late draft (c. 1942), and in successive drafts the viewpoints of several chapters continued to change (thus ch. 9, as Lowry admitted, passed from Hugh to Geoffrey to Yvonne);[6] from Lowry's manuscripts one can see that these changes did not modify the language to any great extent, because complete ventriloquism was never attempted. Lowry makes a few gestures towards varying the style, especially at the beginnings of chapters, and the specific content of a chapter may impose some superficial distinctiveness; but detailed and quantitative analysis of various features serves only to show that there is little objective linguistic basis for distinguishing one chapter from another. The usual effects of shifting multipersonal viewpoint in fiction – interpretation of data from different angles, irony arising from a character's partial apprehension of a situation, stylistic contrasts – are not Lowry's real aim. His method of characterisation, according to his own account, is one of 'heteroplasty',[7] in which the four chief persons are intended to be 'aspects of the same man, or of the human spirit',[8] his object is to create a composite, inclusive or collective consciousness with unlimited resources of learning, memory and language.

In describing the complicated structure of this sentence, it would be more precise to call it 'branching' or 'cumulative' than to use Lowry's term 'overlapping'. It is not built on a traditional hypotactic Ciceronian pattern, with carefully arranged subordination, strongly connected members, emphatic antithesis and parallelism, and with all elements clearly related to a central or climactic clause. My diagram of the main elements is an attempt to emphasise the amorphous sequence of ramifying loosely-linked units, some of them hanging almost in mid-air. The main clause (items 5 & 10) is of little intrinsic importance, but the sentence clusters around it in three large branches (left-, mid-, and right-branches) which in turn lead to numerous other ramifications. Most of these are, grammatically speaking, 'free' or 'non-restrictive' modifiers: elements which are not strictly necessary for the definition or linguistic completion of the unit from which they arise, but which can be added or subtracted by the writer at will.

To begin with, there is a long left-branching construction composed of four adjectival phrases (1–4; the fourth is actually subordinate to the third). Thus the main statement, the subject of the sentence, is deliberately withheld; and the belated appearance of Yvonne in the sentence strikes me as an apt reflection of her hesitation and reluctance to disclose herself. Moreover, the position of the subject in the sentence – detached from the predicate, surrounded by vast modifications – may be taken as an image of the character in the middle of the square, or in the middle of her life, overwhelmed by all the circumstances surrounding her, detached even from her own actions.

After the subject (5), the sentence goes into a mid-branching or self-embedding modification, with an absolute clause (6) leading to a further subordinate element which, without any break of syntactical continuity, totally alters the topic: it moves from 'today' to 'yesterday', from Quauhnahuac to Acapulco, from land to sea (7–9). This ramification leads so far away from the base that the appearance of the predicate (10) is abrupt and almost confusing; but at this point the main grammatical structure ceases, and the sentence runs away in a long amorphous right-branch consisting mainly of noun phrases appositive to 'the square'. The noun is first modified by an adjectival phrase (11), which bifurcates (12–13), with the second fork splitting again into two parallel phrases (14–15).

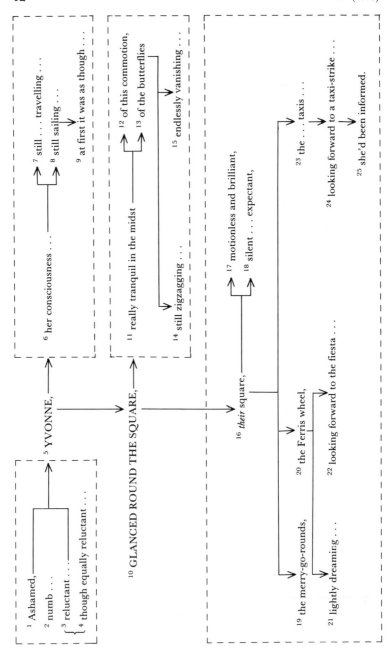

1 Ashamed,
2 numb . . . .
3 reluctant . . . .
4 though equally reluctant . . . .

5 YVONNE,

6 her consciousness . . . .
7 still . . . travelling . . . .
8 still sailing . . . .
9 at first it was as though . . .

10 GLANCED ROUND THE SQUARE,

11 really tranquil in the midst
12 of this commotion,
13 of the butterflies
14 still zigzagging . . .
15 endlessly vanishing . . .

16 *their* square,

17 motionless and brilliant,
18 silent . . . expectant,

19 the merry-go-rounds,
20 the Ferris wheel,
21 lightly dreaming . . .
22 looking forward to the fiesta . . .
23 the . . . taxis . . .
24 looking forward to a taxi-strike . . .
25 she'd been informed.

The noun is then repeated appositively in a specified emphatic form (16), and modified again by two asymmetric adjectival phrases (17–18), before it is particularised by three more appositive nouns (19, 20, 23) detailing its components, two of which lead to further branches (21–2, 24–5). Such a process of continual adding and detailing, of moving away from general statement in a series of right-branching structures, is typical of Lowry's sentences, and it bears implications about his strategy in the novel. The 'logic' is deductive rather than inductive, with a movement away from generalised definition towards illustrative detail; the structure is expansive, avoiding the closed unit from the periodic sentence in favour of an open form with an almost infinite capacity for addition and reduplication. It is clear, too, that this centrifugal development shows a dangerous tendency towards formlessness and lack of definition: this sentence displays some awkwardness and loss of momentum in the final phrases (24–5), and it is noticeable how often Lowry's sentences drift away into an indeterminate ellipsis, seeming to conclude only because the author had run out of breath or ideas.

The amount of matter compressed within the limits of this single sentence is, nonetheless, remarkable. Of course there is no way of actually saying six things at once in language; but if we take the sentence-unit as a metaphorical equivalent of a single moment of time, we can see that Lowry's language mimics a kind of simultaneity. Within his branching syntax the past is merged almost imperceptibly into the present, apparently imputing to the present scene a quality ('this commotion', referring not to Quauhnahuac but to Acapulco) existing only in the memory. That is not all, for two other time-schemes are implicit: the previous year, suggested by the phrase '*their* square' which evokes an old experience shared by Yvonne and her husband, and the future, implied by the repeated phrase 'looking forward'. Thus four scenes are coalesced; each subtly flows into each, within the loose framework of the sentence.

There is a suggestive phrase, attributed to Bergson, in Lowry's essay 'Garden of Etla': 'The sense of time is an inhibition to prevent everything happening at once.'[9] Lowry's conceptions of time were also evidently influenced by the

serialist theories of J. W. Dunne, whose *An Experiment with Time*
(published in 1927) posited the existence of 'absolute time'
containing all moments of past, present and future; and some of
Lowry's long sentences do seem to create a kind of 'absolute
time', an interminable continuum in which everything can
happen at once. His aim was in fact very similar to that of
William Faulkner (of whom I shall have more to say at a later
point), as quoted by Malcolm Cowley: '"My ambition",
Faulkner said, "is to put everything into one sentence – not only
the present but the whole past on which it depends and which
keeps overtaking the present, second by second." He went on to
explain that in writing his prodigious sentences he is trying to
convey a sense of simultaneity, not only giving what happened
in the shifting moment but suggesting everything that went
before and made the quality of that moment.'[10]

This attempt is reinforced by one of the most distinctive
verbal features of Lowry's prose: his use of adjectival
accumulation in long pre-modification sequences, such as 'the
swift leathery perfumed alcoholic dusk' [pp. 49–50(89–90)],
'her guilty divorced dead helplessness' [p. 267(307)], and 'a
black lateral abstract sky' [p. 88(128)]. In *Under the Volcano*
there are about a hundred instances of such series of three or
more attributive adjectives arranged without punctuation or
co-ordination, and although the device was probably taken
over by Lowry from Faulkner (there are no less than five
examples in the opening sentence of *Absalom, Absalom!*,
published in 1936)[11] its function in his work is quite revealing.

It is true that in some of these sequences there is not much
more than tautologous synonymy. Lowry was no believer in the
single *mot juste*, and would not willingly use one word where six
were possible; nor would he have subscribed to the traditional
doctrine of teachers of composition that adjectives should be
used sparingly and subordinated to strong concrete nouns. To
his way of thinking, the bare name of something was a
restrictive over-simplification, and a thing could only be
defined – or encompassed, at least – as the sum of all its
perceived attributes. But although he may not have seen life
steadily, somehow he did try to see it whole. In some of his
descriptive phrases there is an effective compression of minute,
and seemingly disparate, details into a single brief sequence.

Unexpected collocations of adjectives are produced; there is a fusion of an unusual mixture of sensory impressions, as in 'the swift leathery perfumed alcoholic dusk', or of objective description and impressionistic reactions, as in 'the black lateral abstract sky', or of paradoxical attributes, as in 'the numb brilliant jittering city' [p. 267(307)]. The suggestion of seeing an object from a number of different angles is linked to an effect of unity and simultaneity produced by the lack of punctuation and co-ordinators. A phrase like 'sudden intoxicating terrified incidence' [p. 103(143)] evokes a different response from, say, 'sudden, intoxicating, and terrified incidence'; in the latter, there is a pause over each epithet separately, while in the former each adjective is presented not as a discrete modifier of the noun but as part of a cumulative sequence. Hence emphasis falls not on the individual detail but on the series as a whole; the description is not analytic but synthetic, intending to recombine the fragments of hurried perception into a momentary apprehension of the wholeness and complexity of an experience.

Frequent and original similes are another characteristic of Lowry's prose; in particular, it is the isolated comic or incongruous comparison which he uses with so much exuberance and imagination. (The device can be traced right back to stories he wrote as a schoolboy, in which – probably under the influence of P. G. Wodehouse and other popular contemporary writers – he threw off such phrases as 'a peculiarly scaly radiator which exuded about as much heat as a polar bear with frostbite'.[12] Later influences upon his use of similes probably include Gogol and Faulkner.) In these, any object and ground of comparison seem possible: 'Darkness had fallen like the House of Usher' [p. 27(67)]; 'the Consul, innocently as a man who has committed a murder while dummy at bridge, entered Yvonne's room' [p. 86(126)]; 'white sculpturings of clouds, like a billowing concept in the brain of Michelangelo' [p. 122(162)]; 'curious agonized whines, or provocative nocturnal meows, like a nightmare in the soul of George Frederic Watts' [p. 159(199)]. In each example the disparity between the tenor and vehicle of comparison is striking, and perhaps on occasion the conceit is excessively artificial; yet this incongruity is characteristic of Lowry's method. He is not greatly concerned to maintain strict consistency of character, verisimilitude or tone; he is willing to puncture the dramatic illusion, so that the reader has to 'believe and not believe and then again to believe';[13] he couples the grandiose and tragic with the commonplace and absurd, the immediacy of dramatic situation with the detachment of aesthetic contemplation. By yoking together heterogeneous concepts he gives himself freedom to incorporate tangential literary allusions, hints of wider perspectives, glimpses of other worlds outside the immediate Mexican scene or even almost outside the consciousness of his characters. The fairly common nautical imagery, for instance, while having some specific dramatic function (providing an image of escape, cleansing and purification, and offering resonant contrasts between water and alcohol, between the open ocean and the land-locked torrid Mexican terrain), is also an interesting symptom of Lowry's attempt to encompass the widest possible range of implied experience in the novel: the nautical images invoke a whole milieu outside the basic naturalistic setting, and compose a kind of 'other landscape' (to use the phrase of Alain-Fournier, whose *Le Grand Meaulnes* has a rather similar series of images).[14] The centrifugal movement of all these images is perhaps correspondent to the many evocations of flight and escape in the novel – the release of a trapped seagull or a caged eagle, Yvonne's dream of escape from Mexico to Canada, the flight of her spirit towards the stars, the ascent of the volcano; the aim is to get away from the dinginess and muddle of immediate reality, with all its prosaic obligations, and to take refuge in the spiritual worlds of other artists and writers, in witty nonsense, or even in just a simple innocent domestic pastime like a game of cards.

Lowry's fondness for the lengthy and striking simile – a device now fallen into rather unjustified disrepute among serious writers – tells us something more about his strategy. In comparison with a metaphor, a simile is both more explicit and more tentative. A metaphor is linguistically indistinguishable from literal statement, whereas a simile is always marked by a formal phrase of comparison, 'like' or 'as'; yet whereas metaphor is a covert assertion of identity between two elements, the simile retains an open or tentative quality, being merely a suggestion of potential similarity – A is related to B at some point, it tells us, but no more. This vague suggestiveness of the simile suited Lowry, who might well be described as an analogist rather than a symbolist; his profuse novel resists attempts to reduce its concrete properties to definite abstractions. Although early drafts of *Under the Volcano* were crammed with portentous small generalisations, most of these were weeded out before publication as his ambitions grew increasingly large and ill-defined. Where they survive, in such similes as 'Hugh . . . regarded his cigarette that seemed bent, like humanity, on consuming itself as quickly as possible' [p. 105(145)], the effect is deplorable more because of the weakness of the insight than because of the clumsy but well-meaning attempt at definition. Lowry's usual method, on the contrary, is to illustrate an impalpable entity in concrete terms: 'an agony chill as that iced mescal drunk in the Hotel Canada on the morning of Yvonne's departure' [p. 132(172)]; he shuns definition and intellectual simplification in favour of undefined images and correspondences, *'ayant l'expansion des choses infinies'*.

This incurable habit of analogy is built into the character of the novel's protagonist (see, for example, Firmin's ruminations in the Salón Ofélia [p. 288(328)]. 'There is no explanation of my life' [p. 290(330)], Geoffrey Firmin says – or boasts, for he will cursorily reject any explanation offered to him. This is perhaps the very reason for his inability to grasp the simplest facts of his existence; the chaos in his mind arises less from a vision of universal disorder than from excess of a kind of delusive order created by a baffling plethora of correspondences. Everything, to his mind, appears to be related to something else; therefore nothing *is*, clearly, simply and uniquely. 'To discover correspondences in the world around us,' notes Gabriel Josipovici, 'does not lead to the sensation that we are inhabiting a meaningful universe; on the contrary, it leads to the feeling that what we had taken to be "the world" is only the projection of our private compulsions: *analogy* becomes a sign of *dementia*.'[15]

Lowry's way of thinking is betrayed by his fondness for occult or pseudo-philosophical systems depicting the universe as an ever-expanding organism based around some indefinable *primum mobile*. He was impressed by the misty works of P. D. Ouspensky, with their emphasis on the unity of all human activity; by Hermann Keyserling's *Recovery of Truth*, from which he copied out such commonplaces as 'There live in every man, in some stratum of his being, all conceivable types of man';[16] by Annie Besant's description of the Great Tao which 'has no name but it effects the growth and maintenance of all things';[17] by Charles Fort, who conceived of the universe as 'one inter-continuous nexus, in which and of which all seeming things are only different expressions',[18] and whose pell-mell writings show all too clearly his contempt for scientific classification and logical analysis; by Charles Stansfeld-Jones's eccentric neo-Cabbalism, in which life is depicted as a branching tree or a series of artificially connected spheres.[19] Probably this disreputable intellectual background taught Lowry nothing new, but it gave him a spurious authority for the indiscriminate attitude towards phenomena which is so marked in even his best work.

In his later novel *Dark as the Grave Wherein My Friend Is Laid*, speaking through the novelist Sigbjørn Wilderness, Lowry sought to defend himself against criticism that he tried 'to get too much in' his works. Wilderness argues that 'it's better to get too much in than to get too little out', and adds: 'Part of the artist's despair . . . in the face of his material is perhaps occasioned by the patent fact that the universe itself – as the Rosicrucians also held – is in the process of creation. An organic work of art, having been conceived, must grow in the creator's mind, or proceed to perish.'[20] All very well, but the *artist* has to find a beginning and end to this process, and it is an apparent failure on this score which has led to the common criticism of *Under the Volcano* that it is excessively inflated by laboured accretion of material. I do not think that the criticism can be answered simply by saying that such criteria had no place in Lowry's aesthetic; but perhaps it is possible to show, by a brief examination of the linguistic evolution of the novel, that there was some genuine internal dynamism which produced the 'overloaded style'. Consider, for example, the opening of ch. 3 in the version of the novel which Lowry unsuccessfully submitted for publication in 1940. Here Geoffrey Firmin's daughter Yvonne has just entered Quauhnahuac with her friend Hugh Fernhead (I doubt whether Lowry intended the name to mean 'feather-brain', but it is appropriate); the passage corresponds to pp. 49–50(89–90) ch. 2 of the published version, including the long sentence I have previously quoted:

> They walked down a little hill and almost immediately were in the square. A long paper poster strung from tree to tree said: '*Hotel Bella Vista Gran Baile a Beneficio de la Crux Roja. Los Mejores artistas del radio en accion.*'
>
> Preparation was evidently being made for a fiesta. They passed a Ferris wheel, booths, a merry go round. From the Bella Vista Hotel issued weary music; the ball seemed to be still going on. Stragglers passed them, returning home, looking white and exhausted in the morning light. . . .
>
> They went into the Bella Vista and inquired at the lobby. But at the mention of her father's name the clerk, with an amiable smile, pointed to the bar. They entered the bar, blinking in the dusk after the pulsing light, and Yvonne felt her soul contract, as though a car with locked wheels had suddenly skidded to rest in gravel behind her.

In many ways the 1940 version is almost unrecognisably different from the final text; yet the main reason for the difference is not a radical change of the basic linguistic and stylistic structures but a process of vast growth and shift and emphasis. The early version shows in fact the very basis of Lowry's prose, as it was formed during the 1930s in his various drafts of *Lunar Caustic* and in such stories as 'June 30th 1934!'.[21] In these works a restricted plain style predominates: brief declarative sentences, usually composed of a single finite clause; a deliberate lack of connexion between sentences and clauses, with frequent use of asyndeton (omission of co-ordinators) and 'run-on' constructions (unco-ordinated juxtaposition of independent clauses with different subjects); adjectives used sparingly, and most often singly; fairly basic vocabulary; infrequent use of similes and rhetorical figures.

Lowry was always very vulnerable to the influence of other writers. Probably the single most potent influence upon his language during the 1930s was the English translation of Nordahl Grieg's unremarkable novel *The Ship Sails On*;[22] but there were also more widespread tendencies among writers of this period to which he conformed. At a time when some of the most vociferous critics and novelists among Lowry's contemporaries were advocating the necessity for topical, objective and austere writing, his friend Arthur Calder-Marshall was demanding that 'the writer must redeem common speech from loose phrase and thought. His language must be clear, precise and economical'.[23] These self-imposed restrictions may not have been intrinsically wrong; within them flourished a few admirable writers using language more precisely and economically than Lowry could ever do, masters of understatement, of drawing their effects from a deliberately circumscribed range of linguistic resources, distrustful of big words and florid structures. Yet at worst these methods could degenerate into a common twilight greyness and lack of individuality, which Cyril Connolly ingeniously demonstrated by concocting a passage from separate sentences by Isherwood, Hemingway and Orwell in which hardly any stylistic inconsistency was visible.[24] In Lowry's case, his talent lay in other directions: so that, just as his echoing of the fashions of Leftist politics in the 1930s is quite unconvincing, so his efforts to ape these stylistic procedures resulted all too often in sheer monotony.

It would be natural to expect the earlier version of *Under the Volcano* to be more subjective or autobiographical, less organised and coherent, than the final text. In fact it is boringly objective and restrained: a plodding narrative, devoid of linguistic or mental vitality, offering a detached, passive and fragmentary vision of the world. The minimal syntax gives no room for manoeuvre or involvement; it just presents the facts relentlessly, moment by moment, one at a time, without connexion or focus of consciousness. In comparison with this text – or with Lowry's rather halting attempts to achieve simplicity in such later works as 'The Forest Path to the Spring' – the real virtues of the language of *Under the Volcano* stand out; for it is superior not only in vitality and expressiveness, but even in compression and elegance.

When Lowry began to rewrite the novel in 1941, he must soon have realised that greater linguistic resources were needed. 'Not so many paragraphs' he scrawled twice in the margin of the first page of the old draft, thus suggesting his awareness of the need to connect isolated fragments into larger coherent units. By 1942 or 1943 Yvonne's arrival in Quauhnahuac had taken this shape:

Ashamed, hesitant, numbly excited, Yvonne was gazing defensively around the square, 'their' square, brilliant in the seven o'clock morning sunlight, silent yet poised, expectant, looking forward to the fiesta later, the booths shut up, but with one eye open already, the merry-go-rounds only half asleep, the Ferris wheel dreaming – the ranged, rugged, taxis too, that were looking forward to something else their default at the airport perhaps presaged, a strike that afternoon she'd just been confidentially informed.

Compared with this draft, the final version of the passage shows a slight amount of rearrangement (the phrase 'looking forward to the fiesta later' is postponed), a couple of simple word-for-word alterations (e.g., 'glanced' for 'was gazing'), three small deletions ('the booths shut up', 'only half asleep', 'their default . . . presaged'), and, above all, numerous additions. There are some typical modifying enlargements, mainly of adverbs and adjectives – thus 'brilliant' becomes 'motionless and brilliant', 'dreaming' becomes 'lightly dreaming', and so on; but in particular there is considerable expansion caused by the introduction of new material. Yvonne's arrival in Acapulco, which in earlier drafts had been described separately in an earlier chapter, is thrust into the middle of the sentence, yet without altering its basic construction; and if we consider how many elements Lowry gradually added to his text in this way, we can see how the characteristic form of his long sentences evolved. Additional information, descriptive details, tangential analogies, literary allusions, fusions of past and future time with the present: as all these were loosely inserted into the simple basic structure, so the flexible cumulative sentence, swollen with modification and parenthesis, took shape.

This large stylistic change has to be seen both as a cause and as an effect of Lowry's widening conception of the novel. The language grew more complex because of the way that Lowry added new material, draft by draft; at the same time, this expansion was made possible only by the development of an adaptable stylistic system. Among the external reasons for this development, I think that the stylistic influence of William Faulkner is outstanding; and that, appropriately, this influence may have reached Lowry through the intervention of his former mentor Conrad Aiken. Although in a letter of 1940 Lowry made a slightly caustic reference to Faulkner's novel being 'full of . . .

poems',[25] in later years he made a number of admiring comments on his work, and on two occasions in 1946 voluntarily acknowledged some echoes of Faulkner in *Under the Volcano*.[26] In 1939 Aiken published a stimulating essay exploring the correspondence of linguistic and narrative structures in Faulkner's work; according to his autobiography *Ushant*, he began work on this piece while staying with Lowry in Mexico in 1937,[27] so it is more than possible that at this time he planted in Lowry's mind certain notions of the potential expressiveness of syntax which were later to blossom in *Under the Volcano*. After some preliminary exasperated jibes at Faulkner's 'strangely fluid and slippery and heavily mannered prose', much of what Aiken says about Faulkner is so equally applicable to Lowry that it deserves to be quoted at some length:

Overelaborate they certainly are, baroque and involuted in the extreme, these sentences: trailing clauses, one after another, shadowily in apposition, or perhaps not even with so much connection as that; parenthesis after parenthesis, the parenthesis itself often containing one or more parentheses . . . It is as if Mr Faulkner, in a sort of hurried despair, had decided to try to tell us everything, absolutely everything, every last origin or source or quality or qualification, and every possible future or permutation as well, in one terrifically concentrated effort: each sentence to be, as it were, a microcosm. . . .

Nevertheless . . . if one considers these queer sentences not simply by themselves, as monsters of grammar or awkwardness, but in their relation to the book as a whole, one sees a functional reason and necessity for their being as they are. . . . It is a persistent offering of obstacles, a calculated system of screens and obtrusions, of confusions and ambiguous interpolations and delays, with one express purpose; and that purpose is simply to keep the form – and the idea – fluid and unfinished, still in motion, as it were, and unknown, until the dropping into place of the very last syllable. . . .

What Mr Faulkner is after, in a sense, is a *continuum*. He wants a medium without stops or pauses, a medium which is always *of the moment*, and of which the passage from moment to moment is as fluid and undetectable as in the life itself which he is purporting to give. It is all inside and underneath, or as seen from within and below; the reader must therefore be steadily *drawn in*; he must be powerfully and unremittingly hypnotised inward and downward to that image-stream; and this suggests, perhaps, a reason not only for the length and elaborateness of the sentence structure, but for the repetitiveness as well.[28]

It was Aiken, too, who saluted Lowry on the dust-wrapper of the first American edition of *Under the Volcano*: 'Let us all give humble and grateful thanks that we can once again, after a long walk in the desert of contemporary prose, salute a novelist who can really *write*. Malcolm Lowry's *Under the Volcano* must be, for anyone who loves the English language, a sheer joy.' Aiken does well to remind us that Lowry's linguistic resourcefulness can be, at best, one of the chief aesthetic pleasures of the novel. That should not imply that Lowry is a particularly grandiose or precious writer – the rather inflationary tendency of his polysyllabic adjectives and emotionally-freighted abstract nouns is often offset by colloquial turns of phrase and loose syntax; nor that his language is without humane purpose. Since the value attached to language by an author may be an index of his judgment of the subject, Lowry's devotion of lavish resources of language to his work is a memorial to his characters, an assertion of belief, an evocation of times 'when an individual life held some value and was not a mere misprint in a communiqué' [p. 11(51)].

Throughout *Under the Volcano* there are, nonetheless, signs of an ambivalent attitude towards language. In so far as it is a part or symptom of a civilization which is shown to be on the verge of disintegration, language itself is imperilled. The incomprehensible utterances of foreigners, drunks and illiterates threaten a breakdown of human communication; in Mexico, so Geoffrey Firmin insisted, was 'the original Tower of Babel' [p. 17(57)], and the last chapter of the novel is an explicit vision of 'the Babel . . . the confusion of tongues' [p. 367(407)]. Elsewhere, as in several of Lowry's other works, unsuccessful telephone calls provide images of failed and frustrated communication. Even between intimate people, language fails; in conversations between the main characters, true feelings are unexpressed and there is only silence, or laconic oblique statements, or pointless jaunty comments about the weather and other impersonal topics.

In another way, the cumulative effect of Lowry's constant use of linguistic approximators and diminishers is an implication of scepticism about the reality of language. The recurrence of such phrases as 'in a way', 'kind of', 'as if', 'almost', 'somehow', indicates a retreat from clear defining statements; it is no wonder that 'inexpressible', 'indescribable' and 'inenarrable' are among Lowry's favourite adjectives.

With all these escape clauses, his work can be inordinately elusive, seeming to shun any firm commitment to anything in particular. Certainly in some of his writings after *Under the Volcano* his mania for qualification becomes like a nervous tic, attenuating the reality of the work and suggesting a failure of nerve in questions of selection and organisation.

There is a curious method by which Lowry does demonstrate a very direct relationship between language and reality: words, in *Under the Volcano*, can sometimes be metamorphosed into actualities. A simile in which the vehicle of comparison seems incidental, 'the tragic word droned round the room like a bullet that had passed through him' [p. 347(387)], adumbrates the Consul's death by a real bullet; similarly, an image in the middle of the novel, 'he crashed on through the metamorphoses of dying and reborn hallucinations, like a man who does not know he has been shot from behind' [p. 130(170)], is clearly echoed at the moment of his death: 'Now he realized he had been shot' [p. 374(414)]. The opening chapter contains a fanciful description of the Consul's handwriting, 'the t's like lonely wayside crosses save where they crucified an entire word' [p. 41(81)]; in ch. 7 appears 'a stone wayside cross' beside which a man lies in an attitude of crucifixion [p. 244 (284)]. Thus the image is hypostasised; the figurative is merged with the literal; the 'other landscape' glimpsed in Lowry's similes is fused into the setting of the novel.

If this imputes a magical quality to language, recalling primeval beliefs in the power of names to invoke the objects they represent, perhaps it need not be taken too seriously. But there is no doubt that Lowry saw language as a creative instrument rather than just as a tool for describing existing realities. Again I am reminded of a passage in one of Aiken's critical essays (a review of Nicolas Kostyleff's *Le mécanisme cérébrale de la pensée*): 'By far the greater part of any poem is generated in the act of composition: as M. Kostyleff remarks, the initial stimulus, the stimulus which first set the language habit to work, is soon lost sight of in the wealth of other language associations which are evoked from the subconscious.'[29] Or one could say that, in Lowry's case, the initial 'action' of language provokes a prodigious 'reaction', as the introductory approach towards an idea generates qualification, analogy, parallel, and so on. It is better to accept the element of arbitrariness in this process, as a consequence of the unique and dangerous freedom of fiction, than to find ingenious explanations. Given that the novel, although undeniably containing mimetic elements, is fundamentally a verbal construction based on nothing outside the writer's mind, it is questionable whether there are any reliable criteria, except a rationalisation of our own experience of reading, by which we can judge whether Lowry 'put too much in'.

I suspect that Lowry's explicatory letter to Jonathan Cape – the basis for nearly all commentaries in the decade since its publication – has exercised a mischievous influence on some counts. On one hand, Lowry keeps reiterating that 'all that is there is there for a reason'; but the attempt to justify every minutest element of the novel as an essential part of a unified master-plan was really a delusion. By 1949 Lowry had obviously changed his mind about this, since he expressed enthusiasm at the prospect of preparing an abridged version of the novel with large excisions of 'some muddy Lowromancings'.[30] On the other hand, in his insistence upon 'deeper meanings' he allows that we may find 'anything else we please' in the novel, and that 'meanings . . . are practically inexhaustible'. He wishes 'to hint that, as Henry James says, "There are depths"'; but it may not be unfair to suggest that at times there are mere hints at undefined significance. If Lowry could quote Henry James to his purpose, one is tempted to reply with James's comment on Walt Whitman: 'It is not enough to disregard everything in particular and to accept everything in general . . . to discharge the undigested contents of your blotting-book into the lap of the public.'

SOURCE: essay in Anne Smith (ed.), *The Art of Malcolm Lowry* (London, 1978), pp. 72–92.

NOTES

[Slightly revised from the original – Ed.]

1. Elizabeth Johnson, *Commonwealth* (7 March 1947), p. 523.
2. 'Preface to a Novel' (1948), in George Woodcock (ed.), *Malcolm Lowry: The Man and His Work* (Vancouver, 1971), p. 9. This is Woodcock's retranslation of the preface to *Au-dessous du volcan* (Paris, 1949).

3. Letter to Jonathan Cape (Jan. 1946): *Selected Letters of Malcolm Lowry* (London, 1967; Harmondsworth, 1985), p. 82.

4. *Under the Volcano* ('Penguin Modern Classics', Harmondsworth, 1962 & 1985), pp. 299–30(339–40). In all subsequent quotations from the novel, page numbers will be indicated in parentheses within the text.

5. Unpublished correspondence between Lowry and Erskine (14 & 22 June 1946), preserved among the Lowry papers in the library of the University of British Columbia.

6. Letter to Cape: *Selected Letters*, p. 79.

7. Lowry used this term in a review of Earle Birney's novel *Turvey*, suggesting that 'All the Canadian characters, bad or good as they happen to be, all seem to add up to Turvey': *Thunderbird*, 5 (Dec. 1947), p. 27.

8. Letter to Cape: *Selected Letters*, p. 60.

9. Malcolm Lowry, in *United Nations World*, 4 (June 1950), p. 47.

10. *The Faulkner/Cowley File* (London, 1966), p. 112.

11. Henry James, whose stylistic influence is certainly evident in the middle three stories of Lowry's *Hear Us O Lord*, may be another source of the device; at random, I find in *The Ambassadors* the phrases 'a high distinguished polished impertinent reprobate' and 'an isolated interesting attaching creature'.

12. Malcolm Lowry, 'The Light that Failed Not', *Leys Fortnightly* (13 March 1925), p. 167.

13. Letter to Cape: *Selected Letters*, p. 85.

14. See Stephen Ullmann, *Language and Style* (Oxford, 1964), p. 196.

15. Josipovici, *The World and the Book* (London, 1971), p. 299.

16. Note by Lowry in MS. of incomplete novel 'La Mordida'.

17. Note in MS. of incomplete novel 'The Ordeal of Sigbjørn Wilderness'.

18. Fort, *The Book of the Damned* (New York, 1919), ch. 1.

19. See William H. New, 'Lowry, the Cabbala and Charles Jones', *Canadian Literature*, 43 (Winter 1970), pp. 83–7.

20. *Dark as the Grave* (London, 1969), pp. 154, 156.

21. An edited version of this story has been published in *Malcolm Lowry: Psalms and Songs* (New York, 1975).

22. There is a wild confusion in Douglas Day's *Malcolm Lowry: A Biography* (London, 1974), p. 117, where Grieg's translator is said to be 'none other than A. G. Chater, Master of St Catharine's' (where Lowry was an undergraduate from 1929 to 1932). Grieg's translator, A. G. Chater, had no relation to H. J. Chaytor, Senior Tutor of St Catharine's in Lowry's time and later Master of the College. An odd sidelight is that while at Cambridge Lowry published a poem, consisting largely of phrases appropriated from Grieg's novel, which earned the distinction of being damned by F. R. Leavis as 'a curious mixture of Whitman and D. H. Lawrence . . . in the kind of free verse that is hardly verse' – *Cambridge Review* (16 May 1930).

23. Calder-Marshall, 'Fiction Today', in *The Arts Today*, ed. Geoffrey Grigson (London, 1935), p. 115.

24. Connolly, *Enemies of Promise* (London, 1938), p. 106.

25. *Selected Letters*, p. 28.

26. Ibid., p. 116; Woodcock (ed.), op cit. (n. 2), p. 112.

27. Aiken, *Ushant: An Essay* (New York, 1971), p. 350.

28. Aiken, *Collected Criticism* (London, 1968), pp. 202–3. The essay was first printed as 'William Faulkner: The Novel as Form', *Atlantic*, 164 (Nov. 1939), pp. 650–4.

29. Ibid., p. 52.

30. *Selected Letters*, p. 173.

PART TWO

Reviews, 1947 & 1962

John Woodburn   (1947)

Dazzling Disintegration

When I had finished reading this book for the first time, I could not bring myself to set down what I thought of it. I was so much within its grasp, so profoundly affected by the tides of its prose, the faltering arc of its tragic design, a design which gave me the feeling of wonder and beauty and fear, of melancholy and loneliness, the indescribable loneliness I have always felt at seeing a falling star describe its incorrigible curve of disintegration across the face of night, that I said to myself: you are this book's fool, it has stolen you and mastered you by some trickery, and you cannot appraise it tranquilly until it leaves you alone. It has not let me alone. In the street, in my room, where it has set its sorrowful music to the metronome of my clock, in the company of many or only one, it has been with me insistently. I have now read it twice, and the second time has bound me to it more tightly than before. For it added to the pleasures of anticipation and recollection the puzzle pleasure, the story has extended itself as do the drawings of shaded cubes which first seem but four, then, miraculously, eight, and then, incredibly, sixteen. It led me to unravel the skeins of inference and nuance, and the swift *agenbite of inwit* of which Joyce was the cool master and Malcolm Lowry his apt, not aping, creative pupil. Many of these I passed over at first reading, caught as I was in the undertow of its emotion; but the second, returning time, there was still the emotion but it was not the same. I knew it would come, and when, and I could await it; so I had time to wander and watch, and it was then that the esthetics became clear, and the intricate, convoluted architecture was articulated. The first reading was the reading of impact, the war-head; the second was the reading of exploration and discovery, in which the feathering of the arrow is observed, when each of the thin laminae becomes distinct, and the myriad references and cross-references of the book fall into symmetry, and what I had sometimes skimmed as casual detail took on exquisite relevance.

The story itself is dolorous and simple; its complexities are in its radiations. It begins in 1939, in November, near sunset on the Day of the Dead, in Quauhnahuac, in Mexico. Two melancholy, tired and sensitive men, a Frenchman about to return to France and a Mexican doctor going nowhere, talk, over their anís, of a man whom they have not seen for exactly a year: Geoffrey Firmin, once British Consul, compulsive alcoholic, wanderer within himself, an elegant, disintegrating, pitiable and appealing symbol of self-destruction. Dr Vigil has known the Consul for an evening; Jacques Laurelle has shared Geoffrey's boyhood and his wife. As Laurelle walks townward from the Casino in the failing light, he recalls disquietly the events of that day one year before and, inducing still more an already oppressive melancholy, remembers the shy, coltish year at Leasowe with the Consul, in England, when they were boys. This chapter, which has a deep sombreness and great beauty, is of the first importance to the reader, being a sort of epilogue in prologue-place, and containing, as it does, the unobtrusive clues to the story. It is in this chapter that the small tapers are lit which illumine the subsequent narrative. This chapter at once ends itself and begins the story of that day a year before, with a magnificent sentence of elision: 'Over the town, in the dark, tempestuous night, backwards revolved the luminous wheel . . .'

It is 1938, the morning of the Day of the Dead. The Consul, who has not slept, sits in a *cantina*, precisely, deliberately sustaining his alcoholic euphoria. The little foxes of remorse and failure which gnaw at his vitals are drowsy with grape. His wife, Yvonne, whom he loves helplessly and who has left and divorced him and gone to America, appears suddenly, unbelievably in the doorway. A little way down the street is the rococo house of M. Laruelle, who has been her lover, and on whose wall is inscribed, as the Consul remembers bitterly, *No se puede vivir sin amar*. And arriving that day is Hugh, the Consul's younger half-brother, a Leftist journalist, troubled at leaving Spain without sharing her agony. And from this moment, as the Consul's grasp tightens on his glass and his tenuous hold on reality relaxes – slowly, almost imperceptibly at first, the events of that day begin to arrange themselves into a pattern of doom.

Involuted and radiant, the terror and beauty and chaos of

that day are not to be told, can only be awkwardly suggested. Through the fevered, credible dazzle of the Consul's conversation, above his flights of free association, there is a kind of silent agony, of a wild crying unheard, so that one feels that, behind the brittle, brilliant words which divert and assure, a man is falling, turning, tumbling, falling into space.

I tell you, I cannot stop thinking of this book; of the sweet morning ride in the light, cool air, before the heat, the mares followed by the gracile foals; of the dying man lying by the roadside, the horse, already ominous, standing beside him; the swift, symbolic tropical storm, and the odorous jungle; and the scene, like a bright nightmare, in the crowded cantina, at the book's ending, when the Consul finds that all the days of his life have led to that swarming room.

I do not mean to imply that *Under the Volcano* is immaculate of flaws. I do not quite believe in Yvonne; not that she is false, but that she is given obliquely, and Lowry seems strangely to have neglected her. Hugh, who is the Consul's *alter ego*, comes alive for me wholly only in the scene in the bull-ring. I accept the dramatic device of the behavior of the horse in the storm, while I misdoubt its natural probability. But these are so little wrong where so much is so wonderfully right.

There will, I suppose, be the expected comparisons with Jackson, Hemingway, Wolfe. With *The Lost Weekend* only because it deals with the tyranny of the grape. True, it is about alcoholism in Mexico, as a friend of mine said, but it is also true that *Ulysses* is about neuroticism in Dublin. In any comparison with *The Lost Weekend*, and I do not wish to denegate Mr Jackson's achievement, Malcolm Lowry emerges as an artist, to say the least, and Charles Jackson, to say the most as an able writer. As for *The Sun Also Rises*, it was good in its time, but this book would have bettered it then, and it is better, far better, now. Lowry has Wolfe's wild eloquence and bravura, but more grace and discipline and more compassion. On page 37[1] there is a sentence which is 32 lines long and does not falter in its music and can be read aloud without burdening the breath, and that is more than Wolfe ever did for me. Malcolm Lowry has created his own *genre*, and bent it to his will. He is Joyce's own child, there is no doubt, but he is also his own man, an original. There are going to be a lot of new monkeys around now, I tell you, and you will recognise them. They are the ones Malcolm Lowry has made out of some of his contemporaries, the ones who have become our complacent idols, whom we have saluted as truly McCovian, and I feel sorry for them, in their tottering ivory towers or wherever they may be; because they are going to have to go back to their typewriters and start writing with their heads and their hearts and their jolly old genes, the way he does, if they wish to stand beside the author of this book. Some of them won't like this novel, and they'll say so, but they will have to admit to themselves that here is a man who can write a prose that is like wine, who can make the English language serve him like a slave. Otherwise, they had better start ignoring such positive phenomena as wind and storm and the bright veins of lightning in the sky.

I have never before used the word in a review, and I am aware of the responsibility upon me in using it, but I am of the opinion, carefully considered, that *Under the Volcano* is a work of genius.

Ladies and gentlemen: this magnificent, tragic, compassionate and beautiful book – and my neck.

SOURCE: review article, 'Dazzling Disintegration', in *Saturday Review of Literature* (22 Feb. 1947), pp. 9–10.
    For comment on Woodburn's review and on other critics c.1947–62 (including Orville Prescott and R. W. Flint), see Barry Wood's study in section 2 of Part Three, below [Ed.].

NOTE

1. [Ed.] Pagination of 1947 edn; for Penguin 1962 and 1985, the pages are 43 and 83, respectively.

Robert B. Heilman   (1947)

'A Multivalued Poetic Fiction

. . . Oscar Wilde once remarked that Browning used poetry as a medium for writing in prose; modern fiction often uses prose as a medium for writing poetry. In Malcolm Lowry's *Under the Volcano* the overt, external action itself is slight, but it takes on a heavy symbolic weight which must be felt in its relation to the symbolism of numerous objects, properties, occurrences, and even ideas and recollections and observations. The nexuses are imaginative rather than causal, or logical, or chronological; hiatuses compel a high attention; dextrous leaps are called for. In such a sense *Under the Volcano* may be understood as poetic – not in the sense that a mistily atavistic syntax and a half-hearted iambic hauteur, as often in the seeking theatre, pass for poetic.

The 'story', as I have said, is slight: Yvonne, the wife of alcoholic Geoffrey Firmin, returns, after a year's separation, to her husband in Mexico. The events all take place on the day of her return. Geoffrey's passing desires to pull out with Yvonne are overcome by a far more urgent passion for alcohol. A French movie-producer, former lover of Yvonne, is with them for a while and incredulously lectures Geoffrey. Geoffrey's brother Hugh, ex-reporter and sailor, now about to run arms to the Spanish loyalists, in love with Yvonne, spends the day with them. The chief event is an outing by bus – Lowry's own wayward bus ('making its erratic journey'), which stops for a while near a wounded Indian left by the roadside but leaves without anybody's having done anything. Late in the day Geoffrey, who has constantly been getting separated from Hugh and Yvonne, outrageously abuses Yvonne and runs into the woods near Popocatepetl. Yvonne and Hugh pursue. Yvonne and Geoffrey lose their lives by means symbolically associated with the episode of the unattended roadside Indian.

Hugh makes his boat for Spain: this we have learned from a retrospective prologue – the contents of which are certain words and thoughts of the French movie-man a year after the day of the main story. This prologue is supposed to introduce all the main themes; but there is too much there to assimilate, especially since most of the material is not dramatised. It is a cold beginning, and then one has to keep going back to it as to an index – which is not the kind of re-reading that a concentrated book may legitimately demand. Further, on technical matters: the retrospects on which a one-day story must rely tend to be flaccid in style (Hugh's) or foggy in detail

(Yvonne's); and coincidence has a fairly large hand in things. But, once into the story, one is less aware of these things than of the imaginative richness. The minds of the characters are sensitive recording instruments, tenacious alike of facts and of their suggestive value. The book is a cornucopia of images; both the psychic and the outer worlds have a tangibility which a thoughtless slice of realism could never produce; humor and horror are never alleged but are moulded into a hard and yet resilient narrative substance. But one is always driven to seek out the evocations that trail off behind the facts.

So, besides reading the story as story, we are always aware of a multitude of suggestions which, in their continual impingement upon us, remind us of the recurrent images of Shakespeare. The action takes place in November, on the Day of the Dead; Geoffrey feels his 'soul dying'; a funeral takes place; burial customs, the shipping of a corpse are discussed; an earlier child of Yvonne's is dead; Geoffrey thinks he is seeing a dead man; a cantina is called La Sepultura; Geoffrey's recalls Dr Faustus's death; a dead dog is seen in a ravine; a dying Indian is found by the roadside. Always there are vultures, pariah dogs, the noise of target practice. There are a decaying hotel, a reference to the House of Usher, the ruins of the palace of Maximilian and Carlotta. Geoffrey's soul appears to him 'a town ravaged and stricken'; an imaginary 'little town by the sea' burns up. Frustrations and failures are everywhere – engagements are missed, the light fails in a cinema. Always we are reminded of the barranca, or ravine, near the town – a horrendous abyss. Once it is called 'Malebolge'; there are various allusions to Dante's *Inferno*; Geoffrey feels he is in hell, quotes Donne on sin, looks at Cocteau's *La Machine Infernale*, takes a ride in a Maquina Infernal; calls ironically-defiantly, 'I love hell'; at the end he is in a bar 'under the volcano'. 'It was not for nothing the ancients had placed Tartarus under Mt Aetna . . . .' There are continual references to Marlowe's Faustus, who could not pray for grace, just as Geoffrey cannot feel a love that might break his love for alcohol, or rather, symbolise a saving attitude; as in the Faustus play, *soul* is a recurrent word. There is an Eden-Paradise theme: a public sign becomes a motif in itself, being repeated at the end of the story: 'Do you enjoy this garden, which is yours? Keep your children from destroying it!' Geoffrey twice mistranslates the second sentence: 'We evict those who destroy.' Geoffrey's own garden, once beautiful, has become a jungle; he hides bottles in the shrubbery; and once he sees a snake there.

Mr Lowry does not use his rich resources merely to create moods; rather he uses the moods as clues to reality and thus fuses thought and feeling. Geoffrey's tremendous drinking can simply be considered pathological, of course; but it becomes, morally, an escape, an evasion of responsibility, a separation from life, a self-worship, a denial of love, a hatred of the living with a faith (there is an always pressing guilt-theme: Geoffrey, who was a naval officer in World War I, is a kind of sinning ancient mariner, caught by Life-in-Death, loathing his slimy creatures, born of the d. t.'s whom he cannot expiatorily bless but must keep trying to drink away). The horror of Geoffrey's existence is always in the forefront of our consciousness, as it should be; but in the horror is involved an awareness of the dissolution of the old order, of the 'drunken madly revolving world', of which Hugh says, 'Good god, if our civilization were to sober up for a couple of days, it'd die of remorse on the third –'. At the end, Geoffrey, unable by act of will to seize upon the disinterested aid of two old Mexicans, is the victim of local fascists: fascism preys upon a world that has already tossed away its own soul.

The episode which most successfully unifies the different levels of meaning is that of the Indian left wounded by the roadside. He is robbed by a Spanish 'pelado', a symbol of 'the exploitation of everybody by everybody else'. Here we have echoes of the Spanish conquest and a symbol of aggression generally. Yvonne can't stand the sight of blood: it is her flaw, her way of acquiescing in the *de facto*. Geoffrey finds rules against doing anything; everyone feels that 'it wasn't one's own business, but someone else's'. It is modern irresponsibility and selfishness; the reader is prepared also to think of the 'non-intervention' policy by the refrain which echoes throughout the book, 'they are losing on the Ebro'. But this is above all the story of the Good Samaritan – only there is no Samaritan. Devil take the least of these. (Geoffrey's ship, a gunboat disguised as a merchantman, had been named the 'Samaritan' – a comment upon modern Samaritanism.)

Hugh, held back by Geoffrey, is almost the Good Samaritan
– Hugh who is going to run arms to Spain. To Geoffrey and
Yvonne, he is 'romantic'; doubtless he is and he has his own
kind of guilt; but at least he insists on action, disinterested
action. Here we come to what is apparently the basic theme of
the book: man, in the words of a proverb repeated chorally,
cannot live without love. Lowry flirts with the danger of the
topical: the Spanish war is likely to give the novel the air of a
political tract. But ultimately, I think, the author does succeed
in keeping the political phenomena on the periphery of the
spiritual substance, keeping them symbolic, using them for
dramatic amplification of his metaphysic. It would be possible
to read Geoffrey, always impersonally called the Consul, as
dying capitalism, as laissez faire, or as sterile learning, like the
speaker in Tennyson's *Palace of Art*. But such readings, though
they are partly true, too narrowly circumscribe the total human
situation with which Lowry is concerned.

The Consul's climactic acts of hate are a world's confession.
Yvonne thinks of the need 'of finding some faith', perhaps in
'unselfish love'. Whence love is to be derived, or how
sanctioned and disciplined, is a question which the symbols do
not fully answer. Yet it is the effect of Lowry's allusions –
Dante, Faustus – to push the imagination toward a final reality
that transcends all historical presents, however much each
present may comment upon and modify it. Most of all this effect
is secured by his constant allusion to Christian myth and
history – the crucifixion, Golgotha, the last supper, original sin.
Lowry is hardly writing a Christian allegory; indeed, some of
the Christian echoes are decidedly ironic. But his whole
complex of image and symbol is such as to direct a dissolving
order, in search of a creative affirmation, toward that union of
the personal and the universal which is the religious.

The two extremes which are the technical dangers of this
kind of work are the tightly bound allegory, in which a system of
abstract equivalents for all the concrete materials of the story
constricts   the   imaginative   experience,   and   a   loose
impressionism, in which a mass of suggestive enterprises sets
off so many associations, echoes, and conjectures that the
imaginative experience becomes diffuse. It is the latter risk that
Mr Lowry runs. For the present account, though a long one as

reviews of fiction go, consistently oversimplifies the ingredients that it deals with, and it fails to deal with many other ingredients – for instance, the guitar motif, the cockfight motif, the theme of mystics and mysteries, the recurrent use of Indians, horses, the movie *The Hands of Orlac*, etc. Mr Lowry has an immensely rich and vigorous imagination, and he never corks his cornucopia of evocative images and symbols. Some disciplinary rejections, some diffidence in setting afloat upon the imagination every boat that he finds upon the shore, would reduce the distractedness to which the reader is occasionally liable and would thus concentrate and shape the author's effect more clearly. But, if his synthesis is imperfect, there is great power in what Mr Lowry has written – in his solid world of inner and outer objects in which the characters are dismayed and imprisoned as in Kafka's work; and in the implied coalescence of many levels of meaning that we find in Hermann Broch. Such a multivalued poetic fiction, with its sense of horrifying dissolution, and its submerged, uncertain vision of a hard new birth off in clouded time, is apparently the especial labor of the artistic conscience at our turn of an epoch.

SOURCE: extract from 'Four Novels', *Sewanee Review*, LV (Summer 1947), pp. 488–92.

Jacques Barzun   (1947)

'Long Regurgitations'

. . . Mr Malcolm Lowry's *Under the Volcano* . . . strikes me as fulsome and fictitious. Mr Lowry is also on the side of good behavior, eager to disgust us with subtropical vice. He shows this by long regurgitations of the material found in *Ulysses* and *The Sun Also Rises*. But while imitating the tricks of Joyce, Dos Passos and Sterne, he gives us the mind and heart of Sir Philip Gibbs.[1] His three men and lone woman are desperately dull even when sober, and, despite the impressive authorities against me on this point, so is their creator's language. I mean the English language, since Spanish also flows freely through his pages. 'The swimming pool ticked on. *Might a soul bathe there and be clean or slake its drought?* . . . The failure of a wire fence company, the failure, rather less emphatic and final, of one's father's mind, what were these things in the face of God or destiny?' What indeed when so reported? Mr Lowry has other moments, borrowed from other styles in fashion – Henry James, Thomas Wolfe, the thought-streamers, the surrealists. His novel can be recommended only as an anthology held together by earnestness.

SOURCE: extract from 'New Books', *Harper's Magazine* (May 1947), p. 487.

NOTE

1. [Ed.] Sir Philip Gibbs (1877–1962), 'doyen' of English journalism of his time and also a popular novelist – e.g., *The Street of Adventure* (1909) and *The Middle of the Road* (1922).

Anonymous   (1947)

Mortal Distractions

In spite of its theme, the last day in the life of a dipsomaniac, Mr Lowry's book is neither morbid nor of minor significance. If there is morbidity here, it is akin to that of Elizabethan tragedy, born of an involved and passionate interest in the secrets of the fall of man. So strong is the light which the author directs upon his central character that the shadow it casts is one of tragic dimensions.

   In the little Mexican town of Quauhnahuac, Geoffrey Firmin, until recently British Consul there, is faced with the problem of finding a way to an existence in which his wife and he will be free from their injurious past. Isolated by his alcoholic condition, all temporal authority laid aside, Firmin strives against the mortal distractions dragging him from the path that may yet lead him out of the wilderness. He has the intolerable clarity of vision induced by his malady, and the gaze he turns upon his struggle is like that of a spirit looking upon the world. By his strict preservation of the unities of action, time and place, Mr Lowry produces a powerful effect of con- centration. The twenty-four hours pass in the desolate and polluted Mexican setting, with its bars and its bull-ring, its fairground and cinema, and the dominant vision is that of the Consul, his terrible interest in the whole world inextricably interwoven with the problem of his love. In the originality and lucidity with which he has presented this central character lies Mr Lowry's success. He writes with the eloquence of one under the spell of his subject, and, though his manner is sometimes perplexingly elliptical, his central character has the living quality that only great imaginative power can give. He may have set out to write a complex love story, but he has done better: he has created a character in whose individual struggle is reflected something of the larger agony of the human spirit.

SOURCE: review, 'Mortal Distractions', *Times Literary Supplement* (20 Sept., 1947), p. 477.

Walter Allen   (1947)

'A Genuinely Tragic Novel . . . out of Djuna Barnes by Henry James'

Any assessment based on a single reading of so elaborately conceived a novel as *Under the Volcano* must be tentative. Certainly no other novel as ambitious as this story of the last day in the life of a dipsomaniac has appeared this year. It was under a volcano, the drunken hero Geoffrey Firmin reminds us, that the ancients placed Tartarus. The volcano that dominates the landscape of the novel – Mexico, by now one of the more familiar of the seedier slums of modern writing – is Popocatepetl; Firmin is one of the damned, one of the damned, moreover, who might have saved himself but cannot be

bothered to. It is the index of Mr Lowry's success that we are
fully persuaded as, with his ex-wife and his step-[half]brother,
we accompany Firmin through his drunkard's day, follow him
from cantina to cantina in a nightmare bus, pursue him when
he escapes his loving keepers (for that is how he sees them)
through a nightmare jungle to the last cantina of all, where he is
finally and casually shot by local fascists, that he is worth
saving. Mr Lowry, in other words, has written a genuinely
tragic novel of great concentration and power.

   Yet one is not entirely satisfied. Mr Lowry's characters and
his method come to us with too many associations clinging to
them. Firmin himself, British consul in a small Mexican town
until the 1914 war, whose naval career seems to have ended in
dubious circumstances, has been for years on the point of
writing a book on Atlantis. He still loves the woman who has
divorced him out of hopelessness and who on the morning of the
last day comes back to him once again to try and save him from
himself; but he might very well have said:

> I have lost my passion: why should I need to keep it
> Since what is kept must be adulterated?

His dipsomaniac visions and delusions are highly
sophisticated, compounded among other things of
reminiscences of and quotations from Marlowe, Raleigh,
Donne, De Quincey ('that mere drug addict'), Baudelaire,
Dostoevsky, Tolstoy, with some of whom we are lulled into
identifying him. One can scarcely avoid feeling that Mr Lowry
is using the associations of modish Lit. to jack up his tragic
conception of his hero. Then there are the other characters:
Yvonne, his wife, a star in Westerns in the silent days who has
later failed in Hollywood as the 'Boomp Girl'; and her lovers,
Firmin's step-brother Hugh, a newspaperman and a failed
dance-tune writer from the purlieus of Fitzrovia[1] who is
haunted by guilt that expresses itself in an obsession with the
fate of the Spanish Government forces on the Ebro; and
Laruelle, a friend of Firmin's childhood, a once-famous French
film director who has failed in Hollywood and now dreams of
making a film on the *Faust* legend. All, including Firmin, are
members of cosmopolitan Bohemia, failures in the arts,
expatriates. One has met them before in the novels of Djuna

Barnes, Conrad Aiken, Kay Boyle and the other Paris-Americans.[2] They are firmly and brilliantly drawn; their progress is inevitable; but they never surprise; they behave always according to the pattern that the conventions of *avant-garde* fiction impose upon them in the twenties.

Similarly with Mr Lowry's style and method. His style is – one says it with all respect – out of Djuna Barnes by Henry James. As for method, he uses almost every technical device known to the experimental novel, and he uses them with great skill. The book has obviously been worked over and over with the most prolonged and loving care until every possibility of symbolism that situation and setting allow has been fully brought out. In the end, so much symbolism seems to come a little too pat; and, while it makes for an agonising concentration of the tragedy, together with the other factors of characterisation, style and method, it makes also for an inescapable impression of pastiche. The total effect is much more than that of pastiche alone; but how much happier one would feel about this novel, impressive though it is, if one were not so conscious at every page of its literary sources.

SOURCE: review, 'New Novels', in *New Statesman and Nation* (6 Dec. 1947), pp. 455–6.

NOTES

1. [Ed.] *Fitzrovia*: a coterie-label for intellectuals centred on the Fitzroy Square area in London, somewhat self-consciously emulating and up-dating the earlier 'Bloomsbury' model.

2. [Ed.] *Djuna Barnes* (1892–1982): American novelist, playwright, journalist and illustrator; a representative example of her allusive, highly wrought and verbally complex style would be *The Antiphon* (1958). *Conrad Aiken* (1889–1973): American novelist, poet and critic, a friend and admirer of T. S. Eliot and Ezra Pound, and – as we see in the Introduction, above – of Malcolm Lowry, who described him as 'the truest and most direct descendant of our own great Elizabethans' (*Wake*, II, 1952). Aiken was strongly influenced by Freud, who admired his work. Perhaps the most notable of his works in literary criticism is *A Reviewer's ABC* (1958). His autobiography *Ushant* (1952) is seen by many critics as his greatest achievement in prose. *Kay Boyle*: American novelist, poet and translator, and for many years Professor of English at San Francisco State University; a close friend in Samuel Beckett's Irish-American circle.

Philip Toynbee (1962)

Another Season in Hell

Malcolm Lowry was an Anglo-Canadian who died in 1957 at the age of forty-eight. After a public school education in England he became a sailor and wanderer, living at various times in China, Russia, the West Indies, Mexico and Canada. His early novel, *Ultramarine*, was published in 1933. *Under the Volcano* in 1947 – though he had been working on it for many years – and the collected short stories are now published for the first time.

A few perceptive readers and critics have been talking about Lowry for several years, but I confess that I had read nothing that he wrote until last week. I am now persuaded that he was a great writer, and that *Under the Volcano* is one of the great English novels of this century.

Fifteen years have passed since this masterpiece was first published, yet I think we should not be too surprised that many of us had scarcely heard the author's name until very recently. For a novel to force its way above the ruck of its competent, or even admirable, contemporaries, a period of this kind may well be needed. To become wise after the event is the common lot of most critics, and is no great cause for shame.

Lowry was a drunkard and *Under the Volcano* describes the last day on earth of a drunken character who is closely modelled on the author. Geoffrey Firmin is a British ex-consul who has come to the end of his road in a remote Mexican town under the shadow of Popocatepetl. His former wife and his half-brother, Hugh, try to save him at every turning point of the day, but he pursues his self-destruction with as much skill as determination. We are never in doubt that the consul will die before the day is over.

This is a novel about hell, told from within, and it is important to try to establish the nature of the hell which emerges from Lowry's description. Hell is not simply equivalent to an extremity of pain or grief, unless that pain or grief has begun to turn into the sheer terror which springs from the loss of a man's identity. The mystic achieves a willed surrender of his identity, and we are told that this is the nearest that living man can come to heaven. The alcoholic, the psychopath, the psychotic suffer from an enforced and perpetual threat to their identity, and this is the true nature of 'being in hell'.

Yet there is a very strange paradox, which Lowry never forgets about, and this is that the best view of heaven can sometimes be had from hell. For to be in hell is, in its own terrible way, a visionary experience and the man who is confined to hell does share something of the mystic's ecstasy. And thus it is that though *Under the Volcano* is a deeply tragic and often an agonisingly painful book, it is far indeed from being a work of gross self-pity, or even one which leaves us in a state of sheer depression. It describes ecstasy as truly and brilliantly as it describes anguish. It is heroically and marvellously funny – for it is indeed a quality of the best drunkards that they seldom lose sight of the fact that their ghastly misadventures are funny as well as tragic. The drunken man is one of the oldest jokes in the world, and he will not thank those who try to deprive him of his comic aspect, even if they do so out of pure compassion.

Lowry was clearly influenced both by Fitzgerald and by Hemingway, though I believe that *The Great Gatsby* is the only book by either of them which can be judged the equal of *Under the Volcano*. Lowry's prose is far richer than Hemingway's; his tragic and his comic perception go deeper, I believe, than any but the very best passages of Fitzgerald. Sometimes the prose is a little too rich, though this happens less often in the novel than in the stories. Straining at the language, twisting it, inflating it, this immensely gifted stylist can occasionally fall into affectation. But I have been far more impressed by the extraordinary ease with which he forces the language to his own purposes.

I shall not quote because I believe that quotations from a book of this kind are almost bound to mislead. Lowry is one of those writers who take possession of the reader, if he is willing to let that happen, or capable of letting it happen. An individual paragraph depends too closely on what surrounds it; the whole book is formed, is shaped so that each part leads on and leads away again. Yet, marvellous to say, there is seldom a sense of strain in *Under the Volcano*: however hard Lowry worked on this novel, however often he revised, or even rewrote it, there was so much natural eloquence in the man that it springs freely from these tightly organised pages.

There are, of course, other faults besides the occasional excesses of the style. I do not remember a better description of the left-wing thirties than the one which Lowry gives us around the person of the consul's younger brother. Yet it is not a perfect, or even a very good description. (Why do those particular emotions and events elude us all?) Again, the symbols which permeate the book – the Q-Ship which the consul commanded in the First World War; the fiesta; the iron-mine under the garden; the volcano itself – are sometimes a little too insistent. (Yet when I think of them again I must confess that I am far more impressed by their discretion, and by the real service they do to the story and atmosphere.)

. . . [Toynbee goes on to appraise, with approval, the stories collected in *Hear Us O Lord from Heaven Thy Dwelling Place* – Ed.]
. . . the principal fact that remains from all this is that, both in the stories and in the novel, Lowry was a stylist as very few modern novelists understand the word at all. His highly personal tone was carefully evolved through the years not for the sake of ornament, not to surprise, not out of conceit – but because he found that this was his best vehicle for exhausting *all* that he had to say. I had a sense, in *Under the Volcano*, in stories like 'Through the Panama' and 'The Forest Path to the Spring', that this highly wrought style was in fact a marvellously economical and efficient instrument of self-exploitation. And this, of course, is what a writing style should be. . . .

In 1947 a perceptive critic, Mr John Woodburn, wrote the following words in the *Saturday Review*: 'I am of the opinion, carefully considered, that *Under the Volcano* is a work of genius . . . magnificent, tragic, compassionate and beautiful.' [See in Part Two, above – Ed.] Those words will do for me as well; and much the same goes for the collected stories.

Source: review article (abbreviated), 'Another Season in Hell', *Observer* (29 Apr. 1962).

PART THREE

Critical Studies

1. ON LOWRY'S FICTION IN GENERAL

Malcolm Bradbury   Lowry as a Modernist   (1973)

When the post-war English novel comes under fire for failing to continue with the traditions, ambitions, and artistic pretensions of the modernist movement, and for lapsing into literary quietism, there are a few names we can produce to refute the charge. The most obvious are Samuel Beckett, Lawrence Durrell and Malcolm Lowry: writers, clearly, of different qualities and commitments, but all obsessively concerned with an experimental and cosmopolitan view of art. There may be contextual reasons why such experimentalism and cosmopolitanism have had strange fortunes in post-war English writing (just as there are reasons for supposing that a climate is evolving in which in different forms they are emerging again). But that itself makes the case of those writers who have represented and extended the tendency into this era of very great interest. These three writers do have certain features in common; all, like many of the leading modernists, expatriated themselves and subjected themselves to an international range of influence, all take technical expertise and ostentation as an epistemological imperative in art, and all stake a large part of their artistic effort on procuring the right conditions, economic and contextual, for maintaining an ethos of artistic dedication. And, of course, all of them, though they made their substantial reputations after the war, began writing and publishing before it, and undoubtedly take some of their attitudes, colouring and artistic assumptions from the climate of the 1930s, when the internationalist and experimental aspects of modernism survived with greater force and had a direct continuity with the great modernists of the previous two or three decades.

In the contemporary climate, writers of this kind produce clear difficulties of assessment. Though, on the one hand, we have become less confident that theirs is the *essential* tradition of modern fiction, we are nonetheless sometimes inclined to take their commitment, their dedication and the scale of their pretensions as of themselves criteria of literary worth, though of course these can be as factitious as any other aspect of a writer's work. Then again, it is possible in Lowry's case, and probably in Durrell's too, to suppose that the modernist air was not a fully assured possession, was a commitment that divided his power or else stood in excess of what those powers could achieve. An inspection of the *Selected Letters of Malcolm Lowry* (1967), an anguished and engaging compilation of the greatest fascination for anyone interested in the contours of modern creativity, further exposes and extends this problem, which had been growing more and more apparent in Lowry's later work. That collection makes it that much clearer that his work was conceived of as a life-dedication, the dedication of a man of great intelligence and critical instinct attempting a full and responsible achievement. It also makes even clearer what one might also suspect from the work, which we still have only incompletely (plenty of manuscript remains to be released) – that that life-dedication proceeded according to the evolution of a nurtured creative instinct that was always working to place and shape an abundance of material which constantly challenged its producer. One of Lowry's favourite phrases in these letters is 'design-governing postures' – those techniques, often borrowed from others, which compose a wealth of matter already in a sense achieved, but which place and make resonant that matter. At the same time there are numerous uneasy signs of a creative direction never fully achieved: a bewilderment about the potential public meanings of his own type of creativity; a sense, not uncommon in modern writing, that what has been written is not of itself complete, or rightly acquired. Part of this may well be due to Lowry's unhappy dealings with publishers. But the problem strikes deep into his very creativity, and comes out (as it also does in Dylan Thomas) as a principle of vacillation between an extreme artistic ambition and the sense of never having achieved a proper subject-matter to serve it. ... Lowry was a middle-class provincial boy for whom the dedication to art brought a species of suffering, and this suffering becomes a staple of the writing; if one presses personal passions and myths hard enough art will emerge, but as a kind of testimony to one's seriousness. So Lowry can say, in a letter to his Random House editor about *October Ferry to Gabriola*, a book still somewhat clumsily personal in its unfinished, posthumously published form [1971]: 'the bloody agony of the writer writing it is so patently extreme that it creates a kind of power in itself that, together with the humour and what lyricism it may possess, takes your mind off the faults of the story itself. . . .'

Of course this sort of appeal is not worthless; there are kinds of writing – for instance the poems of Hart Crane – where the sense of what literary effort can't achieve *is* so patently achieved that we recognise worth and distinction. But such writing is more obviously romantic than modernist; and that is also very true of Lowry. Though certain modernist features seem essential to his work, his posture in relation to them is oddly oblique, incomplete. One can follow this out, for instance, in the pattern of his expatriation, which for most modernists was a movement to culture capitals, the new urban contexts of art and the centre of new movements and fashions in literary thought. Beckett and Durrell, for example, expatriated themselves via well-forged cosmopolitan links – Beckett to *avant-garde* Paris, Durrell to that and also to Mediterranean life and writing. But Lowry made only the most tentative links with established literary scenes and contexts (in Cambridge, Paris and New York) and rather expatriated himself away from artistic centres and to the idea of exile and voyage itself. When, after spending time in Spain, Mexico and the States, he did settle for fourteen years, it was characteristically in a cabin with almost no facilities built, under pioneer's rights, on the foreshore at Dollarton, British Columbia, inconveniently over the U.S.-Canadian border and virtually inaccessible at times through the mails (a fact which added to the persistent confusions with which his life was bedevilled). He was equally uneasy about identifying his art or purposes with any particular literary centre or literary tendency. He was apt, in the later period, to regard himself as an American or a Canadian writer – but casually and very much, it would seem,

in the mood of his hero in 'Elephant and Colosseum', in *Hear Us
O Lord From Heaven Thy Dwelling Place* (1961) – a Manx author
living in America because 'the people who believed in him were
all Americans, and even here in Europe – once more came that
inexplicable childish pang, yet so deeply he couldn't believe its
cause was mean or unworthy – he'd received no word from the
heart'.

And typically Lowry liked to stress the lonely nature of his
genius, his general separateness from influence, even his
ignorance. In a letter to Jacques Barzun, who had written a
view [in Part Two, above – Ed.] of *Under the Volcano* attacking it
as 'an anthology held together by earnestness', he complained:
'Having lived in the wilderness for nearly a decade, unable to
buy even any intelligent American magazines (they were all
banned here [Canada], in case you didn't know, until quite
recently) and completely out of touch, I have had no way of
knowing what styles were in fashion and what out, and didn't
much care.' Obviously, as the stories in *Hear Us O Lord*. . . make
evident, he was widely read and had assimilated a good deal
from many twentieth-century moderns; there is clear influence
from Joyce (after a Joycean punning bout he speaks, in a story
and also in his letters, of being 'Joyced with his own petard'),
from Thomas Wolfe, from D. H. Lawrence, from Scott
Fitzgerald (whose *Tender Is the Night* he adapted as a reputedly
brilliant scenario, never made into a film). But a more obvious
debt is to the Romantic poets, particularly those associated
with voyage and/or suffering. And his two great modern
literary heroes were characteristically oblique ones – Conrad
Aiken and the Norwegian writer Nordahl Grieg, both novelists
of voyage to whom *he* voyaged in youth, shipping on freighters
to the States and Norway in order to meet them. All the voyage
and journal material of the (posthumously published)
collection *Hear us O Lord*. . . is bound together in a complex
structure of literary allusion, founded on a wide range of
reading from Prescott to Baudelaire, Marx to Wolfe, and some
of it is clearly excessively literary; even so, there is a secure truth
in Lowry's claim that (so he paraphrased his admired Melville)
a cargo ship was his real Yale and Harvard. To a considerable
extent, then, he was the romantic autodidact, and this element
is sharply there in the work.

So it is that there lies, behind the experimental and modernist spirit, a deep vein of romanticism. The signals of modernism are evident enough; the texture of deep literary allusiveness, the commitment to formal experiment, the quality of strain and anguish which itself, as Stephen Spender stresses in a useful introduction to the 1965 reprint of *Under the Volcano*, links Lowry with the other central modernists in his concern with the 'modern breakdown of values'. Yet, as Spender says, Lowry's view of life is individualistic in a way in which those of the leading moderns are not, since through them a consciousness that is ultimately historic and even collective speaks.[1] But Lowry's work is primarily *self*-projection, and the surrounding world tends to be solipsistically merged into that of the hero. Lowry's essential assumptions about art thus tend to be purist romantic ones, art seen as imaginative voyage and representative suffering, all this in the cause of a final transcendence, the fulfilment of a paradisial opportunity. It is against this that he introduces, modernly, a sense of tragedy; his primary themes are then the despoliation of the world by man, and the tragic conditions of the serious spirit in the modern world. His heroes move through landscapes of destruction and waste, landscapes of hell in which symbolic ruination abounds, seeking the restitution of the paradisial garden. To some extent, as in Fitzgerald's work, the tragic derives from a sense of necessary identification with that world, a need to know its nature; and in Fitzgerald this view is supported by a superb cultural and historical awareness. But in Lowry the tendency is rather towards an auto-destruction in excess of what conditions it; at the same time, the imagined world of his books approves the nobility of that destruction. He tended to associate this scaled-up romantic dream of the self with creativity, which he saw as the principle by which we compose our lives. In the later work, I think, he sees the difficulty, and the stories in *Hear Us O Lord* . . . are marked by situations in which fiction, or the created romantic view of the self, is violated by reality; or else romanticism is dissipated by a critique of it, as in 'Through the Panama', where the need for talent to be uncritical of itself is played off against the need for criticism, and a notion of equilibrium emerges: 'And yet there has never been a time in history when there was a greater necessity for the preservation of that seemingly most cold-blooded of all states, equilibrium, a greater necessity indeed for sobriety (how I hate it!).' The confession is surely crucial, and at the heart of Lowry's artistic difficulties throughout his whole *œuvre*. In consequence, Lowry's 'large' romantic heroes, both in battle with the universe and striving to attune themselves to what is transcendental in it, are at once somewhat overly regarded *personae* for Lowry himself, and the subjects of the author's own criticism and even his uncertainty. The result is an achievement that has a fascinating development, an achievement at once magnificent and incomplete.

Lowry was born in 1909 in Birkenhead of upper-middle-class background, his father a Liverpool cotton-broker, his maternal grandfather a Norwegian sea captain. He was educated fairly conventionally but after leaving The Leys School he shipped on a freighter out of Liverpool bound for the Far East, and this experience forms the basis for his autobiographical first novel *Ultramarine*, published after several years of revision in 1933 and then further revised by Lowry and reprinted in a new version posthumously in 1963. In many respects *Ultramarine* is a typical novel of the 1930s. The hero, a young man of nineteen named Dana Hilliot, of British–Norwegian parentage, signs on as a crew member for an Asian voyage of a ship called in the revised version the 'Oedipus Tyrannus' (this is the ship that Hugh sails on briefly in *Under the Volcano*), with a British–Norwegian crew. Hilliot, a middle-class boy cut off from his fellow sailors by his background and his romantic sexual prudishness, seeks the acceptance of the crew and finds it when he finally stands up to and comes into community with the man who has taunted him most. To this extent the mood is familiar; the romantic instinct towards search and fulfilment can only be satisfied by achieving fraternity with his fellow men – the sea invites the romantic search, but only acceptance by the men in the forecastle can provide the field of redemption. But Hilliot's wandering, harbourless, dispossessed characteristics and confused nationality are something that he shares with the ship itself, and his 'wild self-dedication' is part metaphysical: a desire not only to prove himself to others but to achieve a delight beyond despair. He is obsessed by his 'incapacity to position things and see them in their places', and a good deal of the action is in fact concerned with his severance from his father and the need to find his substitute; as Hilliot says – in a magnificent drunken speech, seeing something of the weakness of this – 'I assume the guilt of a mother, or of a father, or of a heredity, imagine it completely to be able on the one hand to give an adequate explanation of my more inexplicable actions, and on the other in order to be clothed in a dark, blood-stained dignity. Some of these points are raised, and you may have read for yourself, in my much maligned and certainly dangerous and misleading work, *Hamlet*. . . .' But it is after he has been accepted by Andy, in a fatherly role, that the chaos and disunion of the ship's machinery, seen as a vision of hell, falls into place – pitiless regularity, interdependence. Sexual love and desire become a romanticised 'sublimated all-embracing love for mankind' but, more than that, a romantic identification with the universe is achieved: 'Then at last again to be outward bound, always outward, to be fighting always for the dreamt-of-harbour, when the sea thunders on board in a cataract . . . .' The gesture is not much more 'than a gesture, but it *is* a romantic one, and it is specifically intended to place what otherwise might be read as a simple political message; what the sea finally gives is not social fraternity but imaginative voyage.

If *Ultramarine* is fairly directly autobiographical, *Under the Volcano* (1947) is so in much more complicated ways. Beginning as an autobiographical novella, its incrementation (the published version is effectively Lowry's fourth) came about very much through events subsequent to its inception – the breakdown of Lowry's first marriage to Jan Gabrial in late 1937 when they were in Mexico, his subsequent drunks, and his experiences with the Mexican police, who arrested him and apparently thought him a spy. Yet the imaginary future that the Consul, Geoffrey Firmin, projects for himself with Yvonne in the letter in ch. 1 is clearly that Lowry led with his *second* wife, Margerie Bonner, at Dollarton. The book also in time came to be placed as part of a trilogy, the Inferno part; with *Lunar Caustic* (posthumous, 1963) as the Purgatorio, and 'In Ballast to the White Sea', the novel lost when his house burned down, as the Paradiso. Malcolm Lowry's two excellent if abstractly elaborate, and certainly not totally reliable, glosses on the novel in the *Selected Letters* – one to Jonathan Cape, who had proposed cuts in it; another to Derek Pethick who was giving a radio talk on it – make it clear that he saw the mythology of the novel as indeed infernal, the world of the ruined paradisial garden, which is hence coherent with Firmin's own auto-damnation. Firmin therefore has no alternative but destruction, since the given universe in which he moves is either destroyed or destructive itself. He is bound to the Day of the Dead – a much less contingent symbol than Bloomsday, at once more assertive and more literary. The destructive cycle is both an historical situation, specifically related by Lowry to the war, and an ultimate human situation; Lowry says the novel is concerned with the forces in man which cause him to be terrified of himself, with guilt, remorse and doom. But what this means is that Firmin's inability to act for his own benefit is a given of this universe. Fellowship therefore lies only in common guilt and common suffering. His search can *only* lead to ruination and damnation; he is doomed from the start because he is a wild spirit. Having thrown up his post, broken with his wife, and acquired advanced dipsomania (Lowry calls this 'the abuse of magical powers'), he can only seek his own destruction heroically. When the possibility of the redemption he desires comes with the return of his wife, he can only, in his state of alcoholic possession, reject it. So he quarrels with his wife, runs into the middle of a dark wood to an all-night cantina, and there meets a group of violent vigilantes – and, encouraging their suspicions about him, accepting their provocations, he brings about his own death in the *barranca*: 'Nor was this summit a summit exactly: it had no substance, no firm base.' At the same time the imagined world of the novel can approve his nobility; for Firmin, 'a Faustian gent', is after all the shattered prince, his wife the broken princess, and he ends the novel clearly as an aristocrat of suffering, a Byronic romantic.

Under the Volcano is Lowry's most consistent work, a coherent imaginative unity handled throughout in a romantic mode; there can be little doubt of its magnificence. At the same time we can see why Lowry must have been uneasy about being totally committed to it, both because it emphasises a 'diabolic' rather than creative view of the world, and because of its lonely self-dramatisation. In a sense the work that follows, notably the collection *Hear Us O Lord* . . ., is a gloss upon it. In the Dollarton period Lowry recast his whole writing plan, conceiving of a sequence of six or seven books, to be called 'The Voyage That Never Ends'; *Under the Volcano* was to be in the sequence, but as a work of the imagination, and the character Sigbjørn Wilderness, the writer who appears in *Hear Us O Lord* . . ., the sequence's central figure. *Lunar Caustic* returns into the canon, but so do other works including the novel *October Ferry to Gabriola* . . . . It is apparent that these books must have been intended to exist in extremely complex relation to one another. For instance the story 'Through the Panama', in *Hear Us O Lord* . . ., is represented as 'From the Journal of Sigbjørn Wilderness' but refers to a novel Wilderness has written called 'Through the Valley of the Shadow of Death' – which is in fact *Under the Volcano*. (Lowry justifies the imaginative necessity for this in a letter; an autobiographical *alter ego*, Wilderness must have been capable of this sort of act of moral courage.) One clear function of this complex mode of presentation is that of distancing Lowry's various versions of himself. In fact *Hear Us O Lord* . . ., abounds in new versions; many of his characters are writers with distinctively similar histories, English, Manx or Scandinavian in background. Moreover a persistent theme is the violation of fiction by reality, so that 'Elephant and Colosseum' has to do with a writer's discovery of literary dishonesty and false rendering, and the multiplying of his *alter ego* figures is not only a means of multiplying his own experience of life and the variety of interpretations he is capable of applying to it, but apparently serves also to soften the romantic core and enable a fuller *persona* to emerge. But the questions raised here must be for an author almost intolerable, in much the same way as they must become intolerable for J. D. Salinger, divided between the ironies of the art-life relationship and a prophetic role. Both writers, in fact, seem to come to the point where modernism – the ironies of the art-life relationship – and romanticism – prophecy and autobiography and the spiritual sense – diverge, leaving a presiding irony. In so far as the divergence is the crucial dilemma of modern art, Lowry's path to it is of endless interest. If, on the way, he left one limited but coherent work, his *Catcher in the Rye*, so to speak, then we can be imaginatively gratified by, as well as fascinated with, the effort. And as for the whole open-ended, self-questioning construct which is his *oeuvre*, that too has its obsessive pull as a mythological fund accrued at great cost and in its insufficiency totally challenging.

If the *Selected Letters* disappoint, they do so by not revealing enough about the quest.[2] But clearly the crucial thread present in the volume is that of the slow elaboration of Lowry's almost mystical notion of creativity. This doesn't emerge as a systematic philosophy, rather as an obsession cropping up in a number of the most illuminating letters (the one to Cape; another drawing a friend's attention to Ortega y Gasset's philosophy; another describing the plot of the lost novel 'In Ballast to the White Sea' to an admirer, David Markson, writing on Lowry's work). Crudely extrapolated, it might be sketched something like this: creativity is an instinct for ordering natural to man, and it manifests itself as a kind of evolutionary force, transcending the reality of nature and giving meaning and mythology to existence. In this sense life follows art. But because this is so, the most revealing aspects of art are those dimensions of it which make explicit the laws and orders that make a writer a writer, and cause him to modify life and create personages. Lowry's own sense of this order was never, as I have said, fully achieved; but it inevitably brought his writing in complex relation to his own biography . . . in which one of the essential biographical facts was that he was a writer. In this way Lowry's heroes are not only figures for himself – and often writers, for his purpose in art is to convey the experience of men of consciousness and conscience – but also are incrementally associated with his previous *personae* and his previous writing. Not only, then, does *Ultramarine* weave itself into *Under the Volcano*, through the in some ways ironic link of the ship 'Oedipus Tyrannus'; so the existence of *Under the Volcano* must be made a biographical or historical fact in the life of Sigbjørn Wilderness, so that the retreat of past imaginings into history can enable the growth of consciousness, the evolutionary instinct. This complex interweaving, this incremental method of creation, is associated with the idea of the writer as the agent of unconscious powers – he must suspect, like Sigbjørn Wilderness, that he is not a writer so much as being written.

In this sense the writer must place himself, by right action, in accordance with some mystical Law of Series, some pattern of creative coincidence that will lead him to redemption. If the Consul of *Under the Volcano* has aligned himself with a law of series that leads to damnation (a view which explains the 'sympathetic' nature of the universe through which he moves), then the hero of 'In Ballast to the White Sea' was conceived of as doing the reverse, and 'in effect', says Lowry in his summary of it, 'both the life of the imagination and life itself has been saved by A's having listened finally to the promptings of his own spirit, and acted upon those promptings. . . .' This is not only a force of life, but a creative operation of the soul, a capacity for identification with a transcendental. Dana Hilliot had found this through fraternity and voyage; Geoffrey Firmin makes a destructive identification; but the hope of a romantic affirmation seems always to have been strong in Lowry's mind. Firmin, towards the end of *Under the Volcano*, becomes aware of a sense of love as a transcendent principle and an upward movement, through which things have greater distinctiveness and separateness – so 'had he desired it, or willed it, the very material world, illusory though that was, might have been a confederate, pointing the wise way'. In terms of the logic of literary structures, the superstitious notion of creative coincidence has of course very great meaning. But Lowry wished also to see it as a moral force, the supernatural world informing the material. In fact it can never of itself turn into a total world view, only provide a posture for one. So Lowry's problem finally lay in capturing the notion of creativity as a genuine coherence; and for this to happen it had to be fully revealed to him and manifested, rather than written about.

But the divergence between a literary and a human transcendental seems finally to have divided him, both as a man and a writer. The romantic dream remains a dream, and creativity comes to mean questions, new starts and new obstructions. Yet of itself the effort – the effort at once to live and to write by an overwhelming principle of creativity – is superb and fascinating. And it is founded on a deeper kind of creating capacity, the capacity, so evident in *Under the Volcano*,

to create a dense and living web of experience, which can give
that effort a literary meaning.

SOURCE: ch. x ('Malcolm Lowry as a Modernist'), in Bradbury's
Possibilities: Essays on the State of the Novel (London: 1973), pp. 181–91.

NOTES

[Renumbered from the original – Ed.]

1. Spender quotes a revealing passage from Sigbjørn Wilderness's journal
in 'Through the Panama' (in *Hear Us O Lord* . . .): 'I am capable of conceiving
a writer today, even intrinsically a first-rate writer, who *simply cannot
understand*, and never has been able to understand, what his fellow writers are
driving at, and have been driving at, and who has always been too shy to ask.'
[Bradbury's italics: see Spender extract in section 2 of Part Three, below –
Ed.]

2. It would have been easy, by better editing, a stronger selection from the
earlier period, fuller biographical bridging, an improved index, and a record
of Lowry's completed manuscripts, to make this the basic biographical
record, at least until an accurate biography appears to dissipate the cloud of
errors surrounding Lowry's career and intentions.

Richard K. Cross   'Modernist Fusion of Symbolism and Mimesis' (1980)

More than a decade has passed since I first encountered *Under
the Volcano* and found myself drawn into a Sierra Madre of the
mind, punctuated by cliffs of fall. Lowry's novel struck me then
(and the impression has been confirmed by each subsequent
reading) as a work in the tradition of those early twentieth-
century masters – Conrad and Joyce, Kafka, Mann and Proust
– whose commitment to a complex symbolic mode did not
exclude, but rather deepened, a capacity for the realistic
rendering of both psyche and circumstance. A narrower sort of
avant-garde writing, the antimimetic, game-playing manner of
men like Nabokov, Borges and Pynchon, has dominated

serious fiction in recent years, but this later movement can hardly be said to have taken the place of high modernism. Novels like *Nostromo, Ulysses* and *Doktor Faustus* clarify the terms of our existence in ways that the newer mode – with its comparative neglect of the relations between the self and the larger world, our common life – has abdicated. The high modernist fusion of symbolism and mimesis has not altogether vanished (Günter Grass seems to me its foremost con-temporary practitioner), but *Under the Volcano* is among the few distinguished examples of it to appear since the 1930s. To rank the *Volcano* with the classics of modernism is to imply that Malcolm Lowry is a very important writer indeed. The disparity between his major novel and the rest of his writings qualifies but does not fundamentally alter that judgment. . . .

SOURCE: extract from Preface to *Malcolm Lowry: A Preface to His Fiction* (London, 1980; Chicago, 1980), p. *ix*.

2. ON *UNDER THE VOLCANO*

Stephen Spender   'Situations which are Self-Identifications' (1965)

. . . At the outset here, I should dispose of what may seem to some readers a serious objection to this novel: the Consul's dipsomania. A book in which for three quarters of the time the hero is drunk may seem too special, too much a case history. It is not, they may protest, about normal life, and therefore it does not concern them. The objection has some weight. In fact, in the last scenes of the book I think that the disintegration of the Consul does – perhaps inevitably – tend to 'take over' too much. The Consul becomes an object, the tragic ending seems too fragmented. But it is only at the very end that the Consul seems his own special case. The fragmentariness of this last section rather serves to underline the control and lucidity of all that happens until the Consul's death. For this is a most lucid novel.

Under the Volcano is, it is true, perhaps the best account of a 'drunk' in fiction. The Consul's addiction is treated as a kind of tragic game, in which there are as many moves as moods, played by the Consul to deceive the others, but still more to deceive himself. The root cause of his drinking is loneliness. The early pages of the book in which M. Laruelle meditates on his boyhood friendship with the Consul indicate this clearly enough. For those who seek it out, the clinical history of the Consul's longing for companionship, his fear of sex, deeply idealistic puritanism, rejection of the world, and suppressed homosexual tendency, is embedded in the narrative. By the time we have finished this novel we know how a drunk thinks and feels, walks and lies down, and we experience not only the befuddledness of drinking but also its moments of translucent clairvoyance, perfected expression.

All the same, that Lowry elaborates the distinctions between beer and wine and Bols and the Black Mass experience of mescal is only incidental to the Consul's real tragedy, which concerns this world in these times. Fundamentally *Under the Volcano* is no more *about* drinking than *King Lear* is *about* senility. It is about the Consul, which is another matter, for what we feel about him is that he is great and shattered. We also feel that he could have written the novel which describes his downfall, and this means that, considered as an art of consciousness attained, this is no downfall, but his triumph.

Most of all, *Under the Volcano* is one of a number of works about the breakdown of values in the twentieth century. Just as the collapse of power in *King Lear* is envisioned through the shattered mind of the king, so in *Under the Volcano* is the tragic despair of Mexico, and, beyond Mexico, the hopelessness of Europe torn by the Spanish Civil War, seen magnified and distorted in the minds of the Consul and of Hugh.

The Consul, then, is a modern hero – or anti-hero – reflecting an extreme external situation within his own extremity. His neurosis becomes diagnosis, not just of himself but of a phase of history. It *is* artistically justified because neurosis, seen not just as one man's case history, but within the context of a wider light, is the dial of the instrument that records the effects of a particular stage of civilisation upon a civilised individual: for the Consul is essentially a man of cultivation. The most sensitive individual, although not the most normal, may provide the most representative expression of a breakdown which affects other people on levels of which they may be scarcely conscious. Yet seeing the needle on the disc of the recording instrument, they know that what it registers is also in some sense their own case.

So *Under the Volcano* has to be considered in the context of the Europe of the 1920s and 1930s which produced *Ulysses*, *The Waste Land*, *The Orators* and other works about the modern 'breakdown of values'.

At the same time it is utterly different from these works, for the reason that Lowry was – to an extent disconcerting even to himself – different as a man and in his approach to writing from Joyce and Eliot – most of all from those 1930s writers whom he considered the 'schoolmasters of poetry'.

The difference was that Lowry's approach to writing was autobiographic, personal, subjective even, whereas the aim of writers like Joyce and Eliot, whom he adored, dreaded, imitated, misunderstood, was to invent a modern 'objective' literature which was purged of autobiographic, subjective elements. Joyce, Eliot and Pound aimed at writing which was 'an escape from', not 'an expression of', personality. Their devices of symbolism and mythology, their attitude towards tradition, their detachment and irony, were all directed towards an ever greater objectivisation. In the consciousness of these poets and novelists there seems the map of an immense landscape with, on one side of a central divide, the order of the past, on the other, the chaos of the present. According to their aesthetic, the poet is an instrument of sensibility acted upon by the situation in which he lives, relating past order to present chaos, exercising judgment, but not communicating his personality. His aim is to create a work of classical objectivity in which the order of the past is re-created, in a form which reflects the fragmentation of the present. The poet himself wears an impersonal ironic mask.

The remoteness of Malcolm Lowry from such intellectualised aims becomes apparent if one compares his use of myths and symbols in *Under the Volcano* with Joyce's and Eliot's. Several critics have pointed out that *Under the Volcano* is crammed with references to myths. An example occurs early on in the book. M. Laruelle, the French film producer, who was a boyhood friend of Geoffrey Firmin, the Consul, and who later falls in love with Yvonne, thinks over the events of the Consul's death, several years later, as he walks along the plateau on which lies Quauhnahuac:

Halfway across the bridge he stopped; he lit a new cigarette from the one he'd been smoking, and leaned over the parapet, looking down. It was too dark to see the bottom, but: here was finality indeed, and cleavage! Quauhnahuac was like the times in this respect, wherever you turned the abyss was waiting for you round the corner. Dormitory for vultures and city Moloch! When Christ was being crucified, so ran the sea-borne, hieratic legend, the earth had opened all through this country, though the coincidence could hardly have impressed anyone then! It was on this bridge the Consul had once suggested to him he make a film about Atlantis. Yes, leaning over just like this, drunk but collected, coherent, a little mad, a little impatient – it was one of those occasions when the Consul had drunk himself sober – he had spoken

to him about the spirit of the abyss, the god of storm, 'huracán', that 'testified
so suggestively to intercourse between opposite sides of the Atlantic'.
Whatever he had meant.

This passage contains a good deal of symbolic myth. But it is
used as metaphor, as analogy. It is not, as in Eliot and Pound,
mythology with which the contemporary situation is identified,
and thus, as it were, within the past, transcended. The abyss
cleaving the Mexican plateau under the volcano, is *like* the
times – the 1930s and 1940s. There is a suggestion of Christ
descending into the abyss for the harrowing of Hell. But it is the
Consul whom we think of here, rather than of Christ. The
Consul is hurled into this abyss at the end of the novel.

A critic – Mr David Markson – points out that the
'all-embracing mythic evocation' in *Under the Volcano* is
'Joycean', and he cites Homeric parallels in the novel, to match
those of Joyce in *Ulysses*. To cap Joyce, as it were, with Eliot, he
adds that this novel embodies 'concepts from Jung, Spengler,
Freud, Frazer, Spinoza, Jessie L. Weston, Oriental
metaphysics –' and, for good measure, 'the philosophical
idealism of George Berkeley'.

This is all very well, but it is misleading if it makes one think
that the mind and life revealed in *Under the Volcano* at all
resemble those in *Ulysses* or *Finnegans Wake* or *The Waste Land*.

The fact is that, though all three writers may use myths and
symbolism and be concerned with the crisis of the modern
world, the aims and methods of Lowry are the opposite of those
of Joyce and Eliot. Joyce and Eliot use particular instances of
modern people in order to move towards, enter into, the greater
universality of a tradition of which modern life is only a
fragmentary part. They use myths and symbols to get outside
'the times' into the past of the tradition. Lowry uses them to
exemplify 'the times', to describe the Consul as illustration
almost. Symbol and myth are used in *Ulysses* in order to absorb
the characters at certain moments into a kind of cosmic
consciousness. Lowry uses them with opposite effect in order to
create the interior world of the Consul. Stephen Dedalus and
Bloom tend to disappear into the cosmos. We finish *Under the
Volcano* feeling that the Consul with all his defects is the cosmos
– and that he is also Malcolm Lowry. This is perhaps a way of
saying that Malcolm Lowry and his hero are romantics.

It has been said that the hero of *Ulysses* is the language in which the book is written, and one would not imagine Joyce quarrelling much with this, providing one adds that language is the history of the race. The hero of *Under the Volcano* is the autobiographic consciousness of the Consul, who is a mask for Malcolm Lowry. Lowry is concerned with the ability of the Consul, conditioned by circumstances which are partly those of his own psychology, partly imposed by 'the times', to wrest a triumph from himself, to create an order out of the material which is his own fragmented consciousness. *Under the Volcano* is not a statement about civilisation so much as an account of one man's soul within the circumstances of a historic phase. In this sense it belongs not to the literature of the 'picture of the West' of the 1920s but to the more restricted literature related to that time and more especially to the 1930s.

In Lowry's novel, the myths and symbols are not mysterious centres of a tradition which lies outside this time so much as usable devices, guides, signposts indicative of the times. They are what the Consul knows and is – a frustrated great man. Joyce permits his characters to know more than they are likely to have known. However we scarcely marvel at Leopold Bloom's knowledge, still less at Stephen's; nor do we think of the mind that permeates *Ulysses* as that of James Joyce: we recognise in it a historic consciousness which exemplifies a civilisation. In *Under the Volcano* we take the mythology to demonstrate the greatness of understanding the Consul. It is a part of his ruinous triumph and demonstrates the tragedy of the 'scholar's mind o'erthrown'. The effect of our reading about ships with the names 'Oedipus Tyrannus' and 'Philoctetes' is of throbbing drums accompanying his funeral procession. The Ferris wheel, the barranca (the deep ravine called the Malebolge) the riderless horse, and so on, are the machinery of his tragedy, itself a machine. They are the Consul, that late romantic, almost Byronic, self-dramatising figure.

Lowry has borrowed from Joyce, turned his symbolic devices upside down and used them for his own purposes either with audacious intelligence, or else from a kind of inspired misunderstanding. But the most direct influence on this extraordinary book is not, I would suggest, from other novelists, but from films, most of all perhaps those of

Eisenstein. The movies – that is, the old, silent, caption-accompanied movies – are felt throughout the novel. Jacques Laruelle is a film director, disillusioned with Hollywood. The Consul suggests to him a subject for a film. Yvonne has been a movie actress – though apparently a failed one. Hugh is a character who could easily appear in a film about the Spanish Civil War or a revolutionary film about Mexico. The technique of *Under the Volcano* is essentially cinematic. The action starts off as an extended flash-back in the mind of M. Laruelle, who, reminded on his walk of the Consul's death, re-enacts in his thoughts the sequences which led to this catastrophe. He then thinks back still further to the boyhood scenes when Jacques Laruelle and Geoffrey Firmin were the guests of the family of an English poet, Abraham Taskerson. There are flash-backs within flash-backs and abrupt shifts from extended scenes to close-ups. The technique employed often resembles cutting. The phrase *Las Manos de Orlac* occurs repetitively. It is on a poster advertising a film in which the chief actor is Peter Lorre. We are told a good deal about this film. Hugh explains to Yvonne, shortly after his arrival: 'I think I've seen the Peter Lorre movie somewhere. He's a great actor but it's a lousy picture. . . . It's all about a pianist who has a sense of guilt because he thinks his hands are a murderer's or something and keeps washing the blood off them. Perhaps they really are a murderer's but I forget.'

This is an example of Lowry's theme-illustrating symbolism, but it also underlines the preoccupation of all the characters with the cinema. Earlier on, Yvonne has described the little cinema in the village:

'It's a strange little place – you might find it fun. The newsreels used to be about two years old and I shouldn't think it's changed any. And the same features came back over and over again. *Cimarron* and *The Gold Diggers of 1930* and oh – last year we saw a travelogue, *Come to Sunny Andalusia*, by way of news from Spain –'
'Blimey', Hugh said.

The words *Las Manos de Orlac* arise naturally enough – whenever one of the characters catches sight of them: a movement of the camera eye glancing at a printed notice. (One thinks of *I Am a Camera*. Someone should write a thesis perhaps on the influence of the cinema on the novel – I mean the *serious* novel.) The cinema-goers' familiarity with this technique is most ingeniously converted into a literary device. Phrases with deeper meanings, *No se puede vivir sin amar* and ¿LE GUSTA ESTE JARDÍN? ¿QUE ES SUYO? ¡EVITE QUE SUS HIJOS LO DESTRUYAN!, are interpolated into the action like subtitles in a foreign language. And of course the technique of divided attention is used to wonderful effect to convey a characteristic of the Consul's drunkenness, his diffused attention.

The cinema is kinetic. Lowry, creating a moving landscape – or a still landscape against people moving – borrows from it for his own kinetic writing. He seems to write with every faculty which is active, or observes action: the calf muscles, the throat swallowing, the frank outward-looking eye observing, the memory re-enacting. In the flash-back of M. Laruelle's recollections of the seaside holidays with the Taskerson family, this fusion of muscular mental energies of body and intellect is seen in its raw state as altogether joyous and outgoing, though accompanied by darker undertones. They are memories which the reader falls in love with, envies, regrets:

These boys were unprecedented, portentous walkers. They thought nothing of walking twenty-five or thirty miles in a day. But what seemed stranger still, considering none was above school age, they were also unprecedented, portentous drinkers. In a mere five-mile walk they would stop at as many 'pubs' and drink a pint or two of powerful beer in each. Even the youngest, who had not turned fifteen, would get through his six pints in an afternoon. And if anyone was sick, so much the better for him. That made room for more. Neither Jacques, who had a weak stomach – though he was used to a certain amount of wine at home – nor Geoffrey, who disliked the taste of beer, and besides attended a strict Wesleyan school, could stand this mediaeval pace. But indeed the whole family drank inordinately. Old Taskerson, a kindly sharp man, had lost the only one of his sons who'd inherited any degree of literary talent; every night he sat brooding in his study with the door open, drinking hour after hour, his cats on his lap, his evening newspaper crackling distant disapproval of the other sons, who for their part sat drinking hour after hour in the dining room.

A passage of this kind has the energy of the life it describes. One sees it all; one could cast the plot which is so innocent and yet so undermined. Singing their exhilarating song 'Oh we allll WALK ze wibberlee wobberlee WALK', the lovable Taskersons, with Jacques Laruelle and Geoffrey Firmin conscripted into their doomed army, walk to Hell Bunker 'in the middle of the long sloping eighth fairway. It guarded the green in a sense, though at a great distance, being far below it and slightly to the left. The abyss yawned in such a position as to engulf the third shot of a golfer like Geoffrey.'

Hell Bunker is also a place where the Taskerson boys took their girls, though 'there was, in general about the whole business of "picking up" an air of innocence'. So there is an underground connection between the Hell of the seaside golf course, and that gulf – the barranca of Malebolge – at Quauhnahuac. Jacques Laruelle one day accidentally surprises Geoffrey Firmin scrambling out of Hell Bunker with a girl. Embarrassed, they go to a bar where Geoffrey, for the first time, orders a round of whiskies, which the waiter refuses to serve them, because they are minors. 'Alas their friendship did not for some reason survive these two sad, though doubtless providential, little frustrations.'

This passage about the golf course contains the elements which are to be found on most pages of *Under the Volcano*. Symbolism is used *symptomatically* to analyse a complex which is part individual, part a consequence of the times. To use psychoanalytical language, the same material of individual and social neurosis is sifted through a great variety of situations.

Malcolm Lowry's view of life is individualistic in a way in which the views of Joyce and Faulkner and Eliot are not. Joyce's characters are – as I have pointed out – instruments through which a consciousness, ultimately historic, collective even, speaks. How they act is relevant in revealing what they are and beyond them what life is. With Lowry one is never far away from the thought that, although there is an illness, there may also be a cure. If the Consul would act, a great deal, besides himself, might be saved, one feels. Thus his failure to act becomes itself a kind of action. His refusal to be heroic makes him a hero, but a hero of consciousness rather than indulging in the Spanish Civil War heroics of Hugh. What seems to him his deepest truth is his isolation. He rejects love to protect this isolation. One cannot imagine Stephen Dedalus or Leopold Bloom doing anything that would alter the whole situation of *Ulysses*. But if the Consul acted, *Under the Volcano* would be a changed world.

Consciousness is for Lowry the effect of individual action.

Through the Consul's thoughts there runs the argument that if
he can attain the fullest consciousness only through drinking
mescal, then he must drink it. Dipsomania is justified, or to be
endured. He also feels profoundly that in these times the price
to be paid for being fully aware is isolation. His dilemma is to
decide whether the isolation involves the rejection of love. The
dilemma is both real and false: real, because intellectually
Yvonne does not enter into the kind of considerations which are
the Consul's consciousness of *terribilità*, and therefore his need
to protect his insight into Hell, in other words his isolation, is
real. False, because his addiction takes too much a part in this
argument, and because (*no se puede vivir sin amar*) there is never
excuse for not loving. The Consul's failure to love is therefore
real: but perhaps the dilemma itself is real. He has to reject love
in order to be alone; he has to be killed because he rejects love.

The desperate isolation of consciousness is absolute. For this
reason perhaps the pervasive autobiographical element in the
novel is inevitable. The author is creating a character who is his
own predicament: and this is scarcely distinguishable from
projecting an image of himself.

The isolation of the autobiographical theme involves also
Lowry in isolation as a writer. However much he was
influenced by Joyce, Lowry thought himself alone among the
writers who were his contemporaries. In the pretendedly
fictitious journal 'Through the Panama' (the writer of which,
Wilderness, is one of Malcolm Lowry's many masks)
Wilderness bursts into a lament:

I am capable of conceiving of a writer today, even intrinsically a first-rate
writer, who *simply cannot understand*, and never has been able to understand,
what his fellow writers are driving at, and have been driving at, and who has
always been too shy to ask. This writer feels this deficiency in himself to the
point of anguish. Essentially a humble fellow, he has tried his hardest all his
life to understand (though maybe still not hard enough) so that his room is
full of *Partisan Reviews, Kenyon Reviews, Minotaurs, Poetry* mags, *Horizons*, even
old *Dials*, of whose contents he is able to make out precisely nothing, . . .

The more one reads his work and about Lowry, the more one
has the impression that he did write about almost nothing
which he had not himself seen or experienced. But that is not
what is profoundly autobiographical in him. What I mean by
calling him an autobiographer is that in his writing he

constructs a picture of the world by piecing together situations which are self-identifications. *Under the Volcano* is his best book because it seems to contain the whole sum of these identifications. The agonies he endured in Mexico provided a catalyst which enabled him to express his deepest feelings about his life, his vision of 'the times'. . . .

SOURCE: extract from Spender's Introduction to the reprinting of *Under the Volcano* (New York, 1965; London, 1967), pp. *viii–xviii*.

Victor Doyen Elements Towards a Spatial Reading (1969)

Malcolm Lowry's principal novel *Under the Volcano* cannot be understood in depth when read for the first time: images, names, printed notices and fragments of conversations often return in an apparently haphazard way, yet with additional details in each new context; different elements are felt to be related though not explicitly linked, and deeper levels of symbolic meaning are gradually revealed. Therefore what Joseph Frank wrote about *Ulysses* also applies here: 'All the factual background – so conveniently summarised for the reader in an ordinary novel – must be reconstructed from fragments, sometimes hundreds of pages apart, scattered through the book. As a result the reader is forced to read *Ulysses* in exactly the same manner as he reads poetry – continually fitting fragments together and keeping allusions in mind until, by reflexive reference, he can link them to their complement . . . . A knowledge of the whole is essential to understanding of any part.'[1] Therefore it is useful briefly to sketch the plot before analysing some of these elements of spatial form.

On the eve of his departure from Mexico, Jacques Laruelle reflects upon a tragedy which happened to his friends, exactly one year before. On that 'Day of the Dead' Yvonne returned to her husband, Geoffrey Firmin – 'the Consul' – whom she had left on account of his dipsomania. In spite of the troubles of

Yvonne and his half-brother Hugh, and in spite of his own longing for Yvonne, Geoffrey cannot abstain from alcohol. His drunkenness leads both him and his wife towards death.

This is the story. The meaning of the novel however is much more complex. On a first level *Under the Volcano* is an account of the individual's struggle for life, of man's fight against himself, against his dreams and disillusions; on a second level the relation between man and wife, the theme of love, is analysed; on still another level the novel offers a confrontation of opposite ideologies, the eternal theme of war and peace, of conquest and fight for freedom.

In their personal life, all the characters are haunted by memories of the past. Geoffrey is brooding over his lost honour. Yvonne tries to escape the nightmares of her youth and the doom of her family which was ruined by alcohol. Hugh is a romantic who draws up the inventory of the – failed – first part of his life. He is an enthusistic communist who dreams of changing the world, but often considers himself a traitor. Even Laruelle, although a minor character, plays his role on this level of the personal conflict. The tragedy of the others has destroyed his last hope. He leaves the country depressed under a burden of personal and universal guilt.

In the novel, however, this personal conflict is never separated from the theme of love and the ideological debate. Yvonne's return is an unexpected factor in Geoffrey's self-imposed misery. He has to choose now between love and drinking, between disinterested extroversion and masochistic isolation. If he chooses love, he has to accept also the consequences, namely complete pardon to Yvonne – even for her affairs with Laruelle and with Hugh – and, for himself, 'admission of total defeat' [p. 208(248)].[2] 'To drink or not to drink' [p. 289(329)] is for this Hamlet-of-the-bottle a question of life and death. His intoxication, combined with a frustrated sense of honour, prevents him from loving her unconditionally. To him her return appears to be a kind of interference with his own personal freedom. When she calls on Hugh's help he suspects them of conspiring against him. The ideological debate betwen Geoffrey and Hugh, in ch. 10, is at the same time a personal drama. Geoffrey's ideological conclusion leads to his personal catastrophe. He claims the right to deteriorate if he pleases, and chooses his own ruin. Since Geoffrey refuses to love her, life becomes impossible for Yvonne too.

The theme of war and peace is always present in the background: the civil war in Spain, the inner difficulties in Mexico, Hugh's defence of the Communist system against the growing threat of the Nazi system. In an even more distant background – so remote that it becomes symbolic for all kinds of war and oppression in all ages – we meet the theme of the *conquistadores*.

This article will show how these three levels of themes are constantly deepened, broadened and interrelated by a web of symbolic references. Perhaps it should be phrased the other way round, because the meaning of this novel is an *a posteriori* in which symbols and metaphors play a constitutive role. Therefore it seems better not to point out how themes are developed on symbolic levels, but to start from elements of spatial form and see how they have a function in the whole. In the first part we follow some threads on their way through this linguistic tapestry. In the second we start from a knot of threads at a certain point and see how different themes are interlocked.

The first paragraph of the novel offers a panoramic description of the setting: Quauhnahuac, a Mexican town situated 'on the nineteenth parallel, in about the same latitude as [. . .] the southernmost tip of Hawaii and [. . .] the town of Juggernaut, in India' [p. 9]. Two far-off places are brought together within one spatial frame and linked to the place of action. Only later shall we learn that there is indeed a relation between them: Geoffrey comes from India [p. 25(65)], Yvonne was born in Hawaii [p. 260(300)].

Quauhnahuac is dominated by two volcanoes, Popocatepetl and Ixtaccihuatl. In the first chapters they seem no more than a part of the scenery; but in ch. 3 Geoffrey thinks of them as 'that image of the perfect marriage' [p. 97]. This metaphor, however, painfully contrasts with the situation of Geoffrey and Yvonne at that moment: he has not been able to seal his wife's return by a marital union. While she is crying in the bedroom, he is lying in a chair with a bottle in his hands watching the clouds that say to him: 'Drink all morning, drink all day' [p. 97]. In Yvonne's mind the volcanoes play a similar symbolic role. In ch. 9 when looking in her mirror she sees only Popocatepetl: 'However she moved the mirror she couldn't get poor Ixta in, who, quite eclipsed, fell away sharply into invisibility' [p. 258(298)]. This description of nature has a deeper meaning. She identifies herself with Ixtaccihuatl (= sleeping Woman), whereas Popocatepetl stands for Geoffrey. But this can only be understood in ch. 11, where the old Indian legend is explained:

Chimborazo, Popocatepetl – so ran the poem the Consul liked – had stolen his heart away! But in the tragic Indian legend Popocatepetl himself was strangely the dreamer: the fires of his warrior's love [. . .] burned eternally for Ixtaccihuatl, whom he had no sooner found than lost, and whom he guarded in her endless sleep . . . .   [pp. 318–19(358–9)][3]

In this context one could also think of *La Despedida*, the picture of a split rock appearing, in ch. 2, in a window with *wedding invitations*. For Yvonne it reflects the enigma of her own marriage:

La Despedida, she thought. The Parting! [. . .] The violence of the fire which split the rock apart had also incited the destruction of each separate rock, cancelling the power that might have held them unities [. . .] She longed to heal the cleft rock. She was one of the rocks and she yearned to save the other, that both might be saved.   [pp. 59–60(99–100)]

This metaphor finds an echo in Geoffrey's comment on another split rock in the last chapter:

And the crag was still there too [. . .] the huge stack clinging to the mass of earth, as if resting on life, not afraid to fall, but darkening, just the same, where it would go if it went. It was a tremendous, an awful way down to the bottom. But it struck him he was not afraid to fall either.   [p. 339(389)]

In these images we recognise the tragic contrast between two different visions of life. Yvonne wants to cure Geoffrey of his dipsomania and save their marriage. Geoffrey cannot accept this. He prefers to disintegrate; he chooses his own Hell [p. 316(356)].

This leads us to another element of spatial form, the *Hell Bunker*. In Laruelle's flashback to his youth [ch. 1], the name of this hazard on a golf course in Leasowe already has a symbolic connotation. After he found his friend Geoffrey there with a girl, they all went to a tavern with the queer name 'The Case is Altered'. 'It was patently the first time the Consul had ever

been into a bar on his own initiative' [p. 27(67)]. In the novel
we meet Geoffrey as an incurable drunkard. In ch. 3, when he is
unable 'to perform his marital duties' [p. 97(137)], and starts
drinking again he notices two old golfballs in the cupboard:
'Play with me. I can still carry the eighth green in three. I am
tapering off.' This is a reminiscence of the Hell Bunker. But we
have to go back to the first chapter to find the link. Indeed, 'in
the middle of the longsloping *eighth* fairway [. . .] the abyss
yawned in such a position as to engulf the *third* shot of a golfer
like Geoffrey, a naturally beautiful and graceful player' [p. 26
(66); italics mine]. In the new context of physical decay and
sexual impotence, Geoffrey's allusion has a tragic impact. In
ch. 7 the image of the Hell Bunker returns. Geoffrey has agreed
to join Yvonne and Hugh in a trip to Tomalín. Still he thinks of
an escape to the Farolito in Parián, where he could drink
mescal and forget everything. In his mind's eye the whole
country turns then into a huge golf course with the *barranca* as
'the Golgotha Hole': 'Over the hills and far away, like youth,
like life itself, the course plotted all over these plains, extending
far beyond Tomalin, through the jungle, to the Farolito, the
nineteenth hole . . . The Case is Altered' [p. 206(246)].

Geoffrey's thoughts are full of dramatic irony: that evening
he runs through the jungle from Tomalín to the Farolito; there
he is shot down and thrown in the barranca. At the same time
the symbolic meaning of the Hell Bunker is directly related to
that of the Farolito, by the allusion to the tavern 'The Case is
Altered'. For Geoffrey the Farolito *is* Hell – just like 'that other
Farolito', a bar in Oaxaca called 'El Infierno' [p. 349(389)]. A
picture of doomed drunkards, *Los Borrachones*, immediately
reminds him of the Farolito! Still the prospect of going there fills
him with 'the greatest longing he had ever known' [p. 203
(243)], for it is the only place where he can find *peace*. In
Tomalín (ch. 10) he drinks mescal, which becomes fatal for
him. His intoxicated mind turns the town of a tourist folder into
a Paradise for drunkards: a white empty mescal city 'where one
could drink for ever on credit' [p. 304(344)], and with no one
'to interfere with the business of drinking, not even Yvonne'
[p. 303(343)]. In the syntax of a distorted phrase Tlaxcala and
Hell are identified: 'I choose – Tlax – [. . .]Hell [. . .] Because
[. . .] I like it' [pp. 316–17(356–7)]. Then he runs off to *his*

Tlaxcala: the Farolito. In ch. 12 he has arrived there. When he visits the prostitute María, the Hell Bunker appears again, but now in a very disguised way:

The Consul's eyes focused a calendar behind the bed. He had reached his crisis at last [. . .] In the dim blue light he even made out the names of the Saints for each December day [. . .] S. Nicolas de Bari, S. Ambrosio: thunder blew the door open, the face of M. Laruelle faded in the door   [p. 352(392)]

But Laruelle is playing tennis with Dr Vigil at that moment! The point is in Geoffrey's free association between the next December day on the calendar – Mary's Immaculate Conception – and that which happens to the other María. But neither is said. Instead we find a colon and an association with a similar situation in the Hell Bunker.

A role, similar to that of the Volcanoes and the Hell Bunker, is played by printed notices and fragments of conversation. The fact that they are seen or heard by *dramatised* narrators is very important. Their interpolation in the text is more than an objective record. It implies not only that a sign *is* there, but also that the narrator is aware of its presence and reacts to it. This however is not to deny that these elements have a deeper symbolic function which transcends the point of view of a single narrator.

In ch. 5 Geoffrey sees a placard on the fence that separates his own neglected garden from the new public one:

a sign, uprooted or new, whose oblong pallid face stared through the wire at him. *¿Le gusta este jardín?* it asked . . .

¿LE GUSTA ESTE JARDÍN?
¿QUE ES SUYO?
¡EVITE QUE SUS HIJOS LO DESTRUYAN!

The Consul stared back at the black words on the sign without moving. You like this garden? Why is it yours? We evict those who destroy!   [p. 132(172)].

Geoffrey knows that 'perhaps the sign didn't mean quite that' [p. 133(173)], but in his inaccurate translation he considers it a warning for himself. In ch. 7 when he has dismissed Laruelle's help and good advice, the sign returns: 'The man had nailed his board to the tree. ¿LE GUSTA ESTE JARDÍN?' [p. 222–3(262–3)]. When Hugh sees the placard in ch. 8 [p. 235] he translates correctly, and there is no indication that the warning should have the same ominous meaning for him as it has for the Consul. After Geoffrey's death however the text returns once more, covering the whole last page of the novel, as a kind of epilogue. Here it is an 'authorial'[4] conclusion, referring to the Consul's subjective interpretation. Geoffrey has condemned himself by refusing Hugh and Yvonne's 'offers of a sober and non-alcoholic Paradise' [p. 315(355)]. He prefers his own Eden: Tlaxcala = the Farolito = Hell. His death near the Farolito is the execution of his sentence.

The biblical symbolism of this sign ¿LE GUSTA ESTE JARDÍN? adds a new dimension to the paradigmatical axis of the novel. The Garden symbol is already present in the first chapter, when Laruelle passes Geoffrey's house and notices that 'long after Adam had left the garden the light in Adam's house burned on – and the gate was mended' [p. 28(68)]. The latter part of this phrase means, on a first level, that the gate – which indeed was 'off its hinges and lying just beyond the entrance' [p. 69(109)] – is repaired now. But at the same time it indicates that the Garden of Eden is closed now for Geoffrey. In ch. 5 his neglected garden is contrasted with his neighbour's. He offers then his own version of 'the old legend of the Garden of Eden [. . .] What if Adam wasn't really banished from the place at all? [. . .] What if his punishment really consisted [. . .] in his having to *go on living there*, alone, of course – suffering, unseen, cut off from God . . .' [p. 37(87)]. When Yvonne arrives home she is shocked by this overgrown garden: 'Geoffrey this place is a wreck!' [p. 78(118)]. It is a symbol of the failure of their own marriage. Even the fact that she and Hugh try to clean up the garden [pp. 99, 70(139, 110)] could be understood as a symbolic correlate of their attempts to restore her marriage. Later Yvonne dreams of a little sea-side shack where she and Geoffrey could start again and be happy together [ch. 9]. This paradisiac image has a striking resemblance to Geoffrey's own vision, described in his letter to the first chapter [pp. 42–3 (82–3)]. But there is still another parallel: the image of her burning dream [ch. 11] recalls also the burning of Geoffrey's letter. Reunited they could have built up their own Paradise. Now they are evicted. The Garden theme adds universal meaning to the tragedy of these two people.

Life is impossible without love. This idea is also expressed in another leitmotif of the novel: the text on Laruelle's house, mentioned for the first time in his conversation with Dr Vigil about the Consul: ' "*No se puede vivir sin amar*", M. Laruelle said . . . "As that *estúpido* inscribed on my house"' [p. 11(51)]. An allusion to this text appears in ch. 2, where Yvonne tries to escape the impact of the words by neglecting them – 'the house to their left with its inscription on the wall she didn't want to see' [p. 62]. The same happens when the Consul arrives at Laruelle's house in ch. 7: 'These gold letters though very thick were merged together most confusingly [. . .] they formed that phrase of Frey Luis de León's the Consul did not at this moment allow himself to recall' [p. 199(239)]. But when he leaves the house he sees the text again. This time it is interpolated: '*No se puede vivir sin amar*, were the words on the house' [p. 213]. At his death the phrase returns when he believes he hears the voices of Laruelle and Vigil: '[They] would set Hugh and Yvonne's minds at rest about him. "*No se puede vivir sin amar*", they would say which would explain everything, and he repeated this aloud' [p. 375(415)].

A poster for a murder film, *Las Manos de Orlac*, adds to the special atmosphere of this Day of the Dead. Already in the first chapter it is a symbol of murder in general [p. 31(71)]. Afterwards it appears at regular intervals along the road* until Geoffrey, Hugh and Yvonne reach the place where the wounded Indian is found [p. 243(283)]. Here murder is concretely realised. 'The *pelado*'s smeared *conquistador*'s hands' [p. 253(293)] remind us again of *Las Manos de Orlac*.

Other printed notices and placards could be added. But we can as well mention some fragments of conversation or recurrent thoughts which have the same function as elements of spatial form.

There is, for instance, Weber's set of stock-phrases. When Yvonne in ch. 2 meets Geoffrey in the Bella Vista Bar, her first words are interrupted by an unidentified voice [pp. 51–2(91–2)]. In ch. 4 we recognise one of these phrases in Hugh's reminiscence of Weber, the man who flew him to Mexico – '*They shoot first and ask questions later*' [p. 103(143)]. The same line returns in Geoffrey's mind during his delirium in ch. 10

---

* E.g., pp. 51(91), 65(105), 113(153), 220(260), 234(274).

[p. 303(343)]. Later, in the Farolito, this Weber turns up again and introduces himself to the Consul [pp. 364–5(404–5)], with almost literally the same words as we heard [in ch. 2]. In the new context we become aware of their ominous meaning for Geoffrey.

In the same way one could describe Dr Vigil's question 'Did you never go to the church for the bereavéd here?' or Hugh's recurrent references to the battle of the Ebro, or the opening line of the second chapter (the beginning of the central story): 'A corpse will be transported by express!' [p. 48(88)]. Let us stick to the last. It takes three pages before the reader knows that it is Geoffrey who pronounced this 'singular remark'. He found it in a 'Mexican National Railways time-table' [p. 51(91)] and during the whole chapter he offers variants on this leitmotif. In ch. 3 he proposes as an advertisement for a new job: 'will accompany corpse to any place in the east' [p. 91(131)], and in ch. 10 the first line turns up in the context of a gravedigger [p. 286(326)] and a railway guide [p. 303(343)]. This theme of the corpse is part of the general theme of Death. But from the very beginning it is related to another element of spatial form, the Blackstone-theme: 'Talking of corpses [. . .] personally I'd like to be buried next to William Blackstone [. . .] the man who went to live among the Indians', says Geoffrey to Yvonne [p. 56(96)]. In ch. 5 he explains to his neighbour that Blackstone wanted to escape from the Puritans [p. 130(170)], 'these fellows with ideas' [p. 139(179)]. In ch. 10 the idea of 'going to live among the Indians, like William Blackstone' [p. 302(342)] returns in his mind, whereas Hugh and Yvonne and all those who want to interfere in general are rejected as 'people with ideas' [p. 311(351)]. Only a dog is praised – 'these animals, these people without ideas' [p. 232(272)]. Geoffrey promises to the cripple dog: 'Yet this day, *pichicho*, shalt thou be with me in – '. He cannot finish his phrase, but when he dies, a dog follows him into the ravine. To the police he maintained that his name was Blackstone [p. 358(398)].

From the foregoing quotations we notice already that the Blackstone-theme is deepened in its turn by symbolic references to the person of Christ. In the Farolito, where a sailor speaks of 'the Old Testament of Mozart', a dead-drunk

Geoffrey preaches, as a second Christ, *his* New Testament, the
glad tidings for wretches – like himself – but at the same time a
gospel of non-interference:

Only the poor, only through God, only the people you wipe your feet on, the
poor in spirit [. . .] if only you'd stop interfering, stop walking in your sleep,
stop sleeping with my wife, only the beggars and the accursed.   [pp. 372–3
                                                                                                (412–3)]

Geoffrey dies in the barranca, to which he once referred as 'The
Golgotha Hole' [p. 206(246)]. In his context of biblical
metaphors a new light is also thrown on the relation between
Geoffrey and his half-brother. In ch. 4 Hugh identifies himself
with Judas because he has betrayed Geoffrey through his affair
with Yvonne [pp. 115(155), 126(166)]. The Hugh–Judas
parallel corresponds here to the Geoffrey–Christ parallel.

To give a good idea of the complex metaphorical structure of
this novel it is necessary not only to indicate different lines of
symbolic references throughout the book, but also to show how
these elements are connected. Therefore we have to choose a
strategic point in the novel and to see how a whole web of
references begins to vibrate when one of its threads is touched.
    The best place to start from would be Geoffrey's delirium in
ch. 10 [pp. 302–3(342–3)]. When we read this passage for the
first time, it sounds like pure gibberish. And in a certain sense it
is. But it is also an experiment in spatial form. When we accept
the novel as a linguistic and literary whole, and detect the
different contexts out of which these fragments are lifted, we
gradually discern, in this mass of loose phrases, the outlines of a
new construction. The underlying emotion is not described but
revealed in a play of associations.[6]
    For practical reasons however we have to use a less complex
example. Therefore I prefer the above-mentioned passage
about the wounded Indian. Here too several lines of spatial
elements converge. Besides the reference to *Las Manos de Orlac*,
pointed out before, there is the horse with the branded number
seven, the theme of the conquest, and what I would like to call
the 'Parable of the Bad Samaritan'. Let us take the latter first.
    The wounded Indian is the man who 'fell among thieves' [cf.
St Luke, 10]; the occupants of the bus and the diplomatic car

are the people passing by. But there is nobody to take care of the man, only a thief to rob him of his last money! When Geoffrey is shot down he remembers the incident: 'Now he was the one dying by the wayside where no good Samaritan would halt' [p. 375(415)]. The biblical name is the link between that incident and another which happened long before: the mysterious death of the captured German officers on board the s.s. 'Samaritan' (a rather cynical name for a disguised warship). Although Geoffrey had probably no personal guilt in this affair [cf. p. 39(79)], the Samaritan-case keeps haunting his mind.* We do not know whether or not he could have prevented that tragedy by interfering. But we do know that he prevents Hugh from playing the good Samaritan in ch. 8. Later he defends his attitude: 'Why should we have done anything to save his life? Hadn't he a right to die, if he wanted to?' [p. 311(351)]. The fundamental contrast between Geoffrey's vision of life and Hugh's can be summarised in two lines of their discussion:

'Why can't people mind their own damned business!'
'Or say what they mean?'   [p. 312(352)]

Geoffrey advocates a policy of non-involvement on the personal as well as on the political level. In his eyes there is little difference between help and interference. A Samaritan may be a disguised conquistador.

Here we touch a second element, the conquest. The meeting of Montezuma (the last Aztec emperor) and Cortez (the conquistador) is praised on a calendar in the Bella Vista Bar as a symbol of the amalgamation of two high civilisations [p. 33(73)]. In fact it is a symbol of the exploitation of one race by another, as the drunken Consul explains to Laruelle in connection with the Diego Rivera Murals [p. 215(255)]. The conquest becomes a universal symbol of imposition. In ch. 10 the discussion starts from the personal case of the wounded Indian and the *pelado* (the thief), broadens into the opposition between fascism and communism, goes back to conquests and wars of independence all over the world, and ends again in a particular case: Geoffrey's choice of personal freedom.

* Cf. pp. 140(180), 188(228), 198(238), 221(261).

A third element is the horse. Hugh and Yvonne met the horse-rider on their morning walk, at a *pulqueria* called '*La Sepultura*' (!), under a tree with a poster for *Las Manos de Orlac* [p. 113(153)]. When Geoffrey sees that same Indian, in ch. 7, the horse reminds him of Goethe's phrase: 'Weary of liberty he suffered himself to be saddled and bridled, and was ridden to death for his pains' [p. 216(256)]. From an 'authorial' point of view this line is reminiscent of another opening quotation of the novel, a line from Sophocles: Man 'tames the horse of shaggy mane, he puts the yoke upon its neck' [p. 7(47)]. When we know however that in this novel the horse will not be tamed but released, and that precisely this act is the cause of both Geoffrey's and Yvonne's death, we become aware of the striking dramatic irony of this quotation which ends in: 'only against Death shall he call for aid in vain'.

Finally we have the number seven, a symbol in itself. In the first chapter Laruelle's Day of the Dead ends shortly after seven o'clock. The action of the central story takes place between seven a.m. and seven p.m. In an allusion to the Indian belief, it is revealed that a cock crowing seven times announced death [p. 354(394)]; at the end of the novel, when the clock strikes seven times, the cock appears also [p. 372(412)]. The number seven has the connotation of perfection. For both Yvonne and Geoffrey it is the End of Time. In the context of the other biblical allusions the seventh stroke of the bell reminds us of the opening of the seventh seal. The horse released by Geoffrey becomes an apocalyptic animal, inflicted upon mankind and bringing death to Yvonne. This is again a biblical metaphor – like the references to Adam, Christ, Golgotha, Emmaus [p. 292(332)] – a metaphor which develops even into a kind of allegory. But this is only one of the various strata of symbolism which give deeper and universal meaning to the personal conflict of one particular man. Geoffrey's struggle for life (and drink) has Faustian greatness. His dipsomania becomes a means of reaching ultimate peace. On still another symbolic level his journey on the Day of the Dead is a descent into Dante's Hell.

In this article the personal conflicts of Hugh, Yvonne and Laruelle have not been analysed; nor has the universal theme of

War and Peace. A few elements only have been offered for a
spatial reading of the novel which brings to light some of its many
levels of symbolic meaning. Obviously this could be developed
further, but even in its incompleteness the investigation shows
that a spatial reading is less a reconstruction of the factual
background, than a descent under the volcano.

Source: article, 'Elements Towards a Spatial Reading of Malcolm
Lowry's *Under the Volcano*', in *English Studies*, 50, no. 1 (1969), pp. 65–74.

NOTES

[Reorganised and renumbered from the original – Ed.]

1. Joseph Frank, 'Spatial Form in the Modern Novel', in J. W. Aldridge
(ed.), *Critics and Essays on Modern Fiction, 1920–51* (New York, 1952), p. 44.

2. Page-references are to the Penguin 'Modern Classics' edition
(Harmondsworth, 1962) – [supplemented by references to the 1985 Penguin
edition – Ed.]

3. [Ed.] The poem liked by the Consul is W. J. Turner's 'Romance',
beginning 'When I was but thirteen or so / I went into a golden land':
included in *Georgian Poetry 1916–17* (London, 1917), and reproduced in many
anthologies.

4. 'Authorial' – translation of the German *auktorial*, as used in Franz
Stanzel's *Die Typischen ä Erzählsituationen im Roman* (Vienna, 1955).

5. Geoffrey's attitude here recalls that of Bunyan's hero in one of the
mottoes of his novel: 'Gladly would I have been in the conditions of the dog or
horse, for I knew they had no soul to perish under the everlasting weight of
Hell or Sin, as mine was like to do [p. 7(47)].

6. Apart from being the most difficult and most experimental, ch. 10 is also
the best of the novel. To prove this in a few lines, however, is impossible. One
might think of the confusing structure, which is the correlate of Geoffrey's
confused point of view; the integration of heterogeneous elements (tourist
folder, timetable); the mixture of dream and reality; the growing symbolism
of Tlaxcala; the universalisation of the theme of War and Peace; and
Geoffrey's conclusion for his own life.

Dale Edmonds A Mosaic of Doom: A Reading of the 'Immediate Level' (1968)

. . . The Consul's murder at the *Farolito* in Parián is not a trick, but is the outcome of a series of interrelated circumstances, depending upon the Consul's past, his role in Quauhnahuac, and conditions in Mexico during the time of the novel's action. Careful scrutiny reveals that the events of chs 2–12 form an intricate mosaic of doom for the Consul. This mosaic is formed upon a background of the political situation in Mexico in 1938–39. Because many of the occurrences in the novel fail to make full sense without an awareness of this background, I shall summarise it briefly.

Mexico in the mid- and late 1930s was in a state of turmoil. In addition to internal difficulties, foreign communist and fascist interests sought to influence affairs in Mexico.[1] Lázaro Cárdenas, elected president of Mexico in July of 1934, proved himself a different man from what Plutarco Elias Calles expected when he selected Cárdenas as presidential candidate (Calles had been the power behind the Mexican political scene since 1928 when he left the presidency). Under Cárdenas Calles had hoped to retain virtual control of the government, as he had during the presidencies of Emilio Portes Gil, Pascual Órtiz Rubio and Abelardo Rodríguez. But, according to Henry Bamford Parkes, in *A History of Mexico*,[2] Calles 'discovered that he had supplied the left wing not merely with a figurehead but with a leader. Cárdenas proved himself not only a man of integrity but also a remarkably able politician' [p. 400]. In April 1936, to avoid possible trouble, Cárdenas deported Calles to the United States. 'To American newspapermen', Parkes writes [p. 401], 'Calles explained that he had been banished because he was an enemy of Communism, and it was observed that he was carrying a copy of Hitler's *Mein Kampf.*'

Strong support for Cárdenas came from labor, including a federation of labor unions formed in 1936 called *Confederación de Trabajadores de Mexico*, or CTM. Another source of support for

Cárdenas was the small farmer. One of his most important policies was a firm and energetic program of agrarian reform – anathema to the Callistas and other reactionary elements in Mexico. According to Parkes [p. 403], 'By 1940 [Cárdenas] had distributed forty-five million acres of land . . . among three quarters of a million peasant families located in nearly twelve thousand different villages.' Obviously such a program antagonised wealthy hacienda owners who watched their holdings being pared away. Under Cárdenas, Parkes writes [p. 407], 'the agrarian reform included not merely the distribution of plots of ground upon which peasants could grow corn, but also the organisation of large co-operative farms for the production of commercial crops on a profit-sharing basis'. The *ejido*, a tract of common land for a village, had been a Mexican institution since pre-Cortesian days, but the institution often was abused or ignored altogether. Cárdenas breathed new life into the *ejido* concept. The money for financing the operation of the new *ejido* concept was administered through the *National Bank of Ejido Credit*, an institution that will figure in an important way in *Under the Volcano*.

Although Cárdenas's collectivist sympathies should be apparent from the foregoing discussion, he was not a doctrinaire socialist, nor was he, as his enemies charged, a communist. Perhaps his most controversial act was his expropriation of foreign oil companies in March 1938, following the refusal of these companies to answer government demands for increasing wages and training native Mexicans for managerial positions. The British government protested against the expropriation, with the result that diplomatic relations between the two countries ceased in the spring of 1938.

Nazi Germany had good reason for being interested in Mexico: opposition to Cárdenas was strong enough to indicate that Germany might be able to help overthrow him and thereby gain a toehold in the Western hemisphere. As a result of Germany's interest, Parkes relates [p. 409], 'there was a marked growth of reactionary and fascistic groups who were encouraged by German agents and assisted by German money. These forces received further stimulus from the victory of

Franco in the Spanish Civil War'. Cárdenas and his
government were outspokenly pro-Loyalist, another attitude
that antagonised reactionary elements in Mexico. Among the
extreme rightist groups that came into existence in the late
1930s was the *Unión Nacional Sinarquista*, which received
encouragement from the Spanish Falange and probably from
Nazi Germany. The *Unión Militar* of *Under the Volcano* seems to
be an arm of such an organisation. One of the chief targets of
the rightist organisations was Cárdenas's agrarian reform
program, and the agencies and individuals by which it was
administered. In *Under the Volcano*, the *National Bank of Ejido
Credit* is such an agency, and the Indian who rode the horse
with the number '7' branded on its rump is such an individual.

The foregoing sketch of the political situation in Mexico in
the mid- and late 1930s suggests the actual background for
some of the more important events in *Under the Volcano*, a
background with which Lowry was familiar from his residence
in Mexico.[3] But the important point here is neither
biographical nor historical: Lowry used details from the
Mexican political situation in his intricate development of the
story of *Under the Volcano*.

Several critics have remarked that after finishing *Under the
Volcano* one should immediately re-read the first chapter; and so
one should because ch. 1 resolves a number of apparently
puzzling questions raised in chs 2–12. Jacques, Dr Vigil, and
Señor Bustamente have had a year in which to reflect on the
events of the Day of the Dead in 1938, and the political situation
has come into sharper focus. Particularly important in ch. 1 is
material about the Consul's political role in Quauhnahuac and
how this role related to the events leading to his death.

Shortly after dusk on the Day of the Dead in 1939, a year after
the Consul's death, Jacques and Señor Bustamente, manager of
the cinema, sit in the *Cervecería XX* next door to the cinema and
discuss the Consul. The immediate impetus of their discussion
is the Consul's volume of Elizabethan plays which Bustamente
has just returned to Jacques (Jacques left it in the cinema the
day he borrowed it, some eighteen months before). This
conversation between Jacques and Bustamente is extremely
important for the interpretation of events it suggests, although

Lowry deliberately presents this material in a tentative and speculative way, not insisting on any one interpretation. In much of Lowry's fiction we can never be certain that we are dealing with reality (in terms of the fictional world created), with the result that any conclusions we draw must consider the enigmatic nature of the material. In the analysis which follows I do not ignore the possibility that Bustamente's suspicions may be unfounded, but I also do not ignore the possibility that Jacques's refutation of these suspicions may be unfounded.

Bustamente remembers the days of Porfirio Díaz when every small American border town harbored a Mexican 'Consul'; indeed, Mexican consuls even were found in towns some distance from the border. These Consuls supposedly looked after interests of trade between Mexico and the United States, but this was merely a front, as most were spies for the Díaz regime. Bustamente hints, 'without offence, and perhaps not altogether seriously', that Geoffrey Firmin had been such a Consul – a British Consul, of course, but one 'who could scarcely claim to have the interests of British trade at heart in a place where there were no British interests and no Englishmen, the less so when it was considered that England had severed diplomatic relations with Mexico' [p. 36(76)] Bustamente seems half-convinced that Jacques has been taken in, that the Consul really was a 'spider' (as he, and other Mexicans in the book, express the English word 'spy').

Then comes an important passage, actually a reflection by Jacques generated by Bustamente's expression of sympathy for the Consul: '. . . [the Consul wandered] hatless and desconsolado and beside himself around the town pursued by other spiders who, without his ever being quite certain of it, a man in dark glasses he took to be a loafer here, a man lounging on the other side of the road he thought was a peon there, a bald boy with earrings swinging madly on a creaking hammock there, guarded every street and alley entrance . . .' [p. 36(76)]. Each of these possible 'counter-spiders' appears at least once in the course of the narrative in chs 2–12; the man with dark glasses appears several times.

The impression the Consul gave Bustamente was a man living in continual terror of his life, for reasons more tangible than alcoholic hallucination. After Jacques, by citing the

Consul's war record, has pointed out that the Consul was not a coward, Bustamente agrees, then explains the difference in Mexico between fearing for one's life and being a coward. Bustamente suggests, 'might not just such a character and distinguished record as M. Laruelle claimed was his [the Consul's] have precisely qualified him for the excessively dangerous activities of a spider?' [p. 37(77)]. These qualities might – but then again, they might not, Jacques believes. He thinks it useless to try to explain to Bustamente that the Consul's job in Quauhnahuac was 'merely a retreat . . . a position where he was least likely to prove a nuisance to the Empire . . .' [p. 32]. This is so of the Consul's official post – but what of his activities that were not included in the specific duties of a British Consul? From my earlier discussion of the political situation in Mexico at the time, it should be clear that ample opportunity existed for all manner of espionage activities.[4] If German agents were so active in Mexico, British agents might have been similarly active. Of the Consul's precise duties as a British spy (if he is one) we never learn, but we may assume that they included keeping his eyes open for, and reporting upon, any suspicious individuals or activities – specifically fascist – he observed.

Britain's position in regard to Mexico was paradoxical: on the one hand, she resented Mexico's expropriation of her oil companies; on the other hand, she sympathised with certain of Cárdenas' aims (such as equitable land distribution) which fascist forces would have opposed. The situation might be described in this manner: the fascist agents – including, perhaps, the Consul – were not so much pro-Cárdenas as they were, simply, pro-British, concerned with anything that might in some way affect the interests of the British Empire.

The Consul's role in Quauhnahuac at the time the events of chs 2–12 take place may be summarised as follows: he no longer is officially British Consul (after breaking off diplomatic relations with Mexico, Britain called her Consuls home), but remains to 'look after the interests' of his country, which he does, primarily, by reporting fascist activities. The events of chs 2–12 corroborate this view.[5]

It is 7:00 a.m. on the Day of the Dead in 1938, with Yvonne
Firmin standing outside the bar of the *Bella Vista Hotel.* She has
just flown to Quauhnahuac on the little red mail plane from
Acapulco, and has been brought to this spot by a station wagon
from the air field: 'A corpse will be transported by express!'
Yvonne hears someone say inside the bar [p. 48(88)].
Recognising her ex-husband's voice, Yvonne tries to gather the
courage to go inside. Another voice, which she doesn't
recognise, exclaims, ' – *just a bunch of Alladamnbama farmers!*'.
This is the voice of Weber, the 'American semi-fascist', as
Hugh calls him, who has flown with Hugh into Quauhnahuac
[p. 103(143)]. Thus the political note is sounded at the outset of
the novel's main narrative portion, for both Weber himself and
what he represents are to reappear again during the day. The
Consul has described Weber as a 'gun-running gun-toting pal'
of Hugh's; Hugh later tells Yvonne that he strongly suspects
Weber of running ammunition to the *Unión Militar* and possibly
to other pro-fascist, anti-Cárdenas special police groups
[p. 65(105)]. Hugh had argued with Weber in a dive in El Paso,
then later had ridden with him in a cattle truck to Chihuahua,
and from there, had flown with him to Quauhnahuac. Parián,
though, is where Weber wants to go – 'I wonder what Weber
sees in it', Hugh asks [p. 119(159)]. What Weber 'sees' in
Parián is the headquarters of the *Unión Militar,* where he is to
make some sort of connection concerning his smuggling deals,
perhaps to deliver or collect for a shipment. At the *Salón Ofélia*
in ch. 10 Hugh mentions to Yvonne the large number of Nazis
and fascists in Mexico, and remarks that 'pubs' make ideal
headquarters for their activities, 'In the Pilsener Kindl, for
instance, in Mexico City – [p. 300(340)]. The Consul
interposes, unheard from his seat in the toilet, 'Not to mention
in Parián, Hugh. . . . In the Farolito –'. In ch. 12, at the
Farolito, Weber refuses to intervene to save the Consul. After
reading Hugh's telegram which was still in the pocket of the
Consul's tweed jacket Hugh had borrowed earlier, one of the
policemen asks the Consul why he said his name was
Blackstone since 'It say here too: Your name is Firmin'. It
strikes the Consul that Weber is 'staring at him with a remote
speculation'. Weber could have pointed out that the telegram
was Hugh's, not the Consul's; he could, at least, have identified

the Consul – Hugh must have told Weber about his half-brother. But Weber does nothing, perhaps assuming that anything that happens to a Firmin will be a blow to a leftist cause. Although Weber does not contribute positively to the Consul's death, we might regard his failure to intervene as a negative contribution.

There is no doubt about where Weber stands. With a number of other minor characters we are not so certain. Returning to the morning scene in the *Bella Vista Hotel*, we find one such character here, the old Tarascan woman with the dominoes, whom the Consul points out to Yvonne. To Yvonne the old woman, with her dominoes and her chicken on a cord, seems an evil omen, but it becomes clear later that the old woman is sympathetic with the Consul; in fact, she may be in some vague way an anti-fascist 'spider'. In the arena at Tomalín, Yvonne, repairing her make-up, notices behind her, reflected in her compact mirror, Popocatepetl. Then, 'For a second she'd had the awful sensation that, not Popocatepetl, but the old woman with the dominoes that morning was looking over her shoulder' [p. 258(298)]. This may be more than an illusion on Yvonne's part, for we find the old woman later at the *Farolito*. She would pass through Tomalín on her way to Parián, and it is possible she may have gone briefly to the arena. It is also possible that her appearance there may be connected with the Consul's presence, for her subsequent actions indicate that her concern for his safety is something more than desultory interest. At the *Farolito*, the Consul takes his drink and Yvonne's letters into an inner room where 'he was not really surprised to find the old Tarascan woman . . .' [p. 344(384)]. The Consul familiarly settles beside her to read his letters. As the *fascistas* decide the Consul's fate with their telephone call, the old Tarascan woman appears once more. 'No good for you', she whispers to him, 'Bad place. Muy malo. These man no friend of Mexican people. . . . They no policia. They diablos. Murderers' [p. 368(408)]. But the Consul only raises his glass, 'Gracias, buena amiga', and she leaves. Moments later the old woman loyally appears once more, but can only shake her head and frown sadly, for the Consul is beyond help. Lowry, then, seems to be hinting rather broadly that this old woman is a benevolent 'familiar'.

Other 'familiars' watch the Consul with undeniably malevolent intent. There is considerable evidence to suggest that these 'counter-spiders' are employed to keep their eyes on the Consul, to follow his movements, and to report on his activities to those who pay their salaries. The most active of these 'counter-spiders', the 'man in dark glasses', to whom Bustamente and Jacques have referred in ch. 1, appears early in ch. 2. Yvonne and the Consul leave the bar of the *Bella Vista* a little after 7:00 a.m.: 'So confused by apprehension of meeting any acquaintance was she, Yvonne had almost taken the arm of another man wearing dark glasses, a ragged young Mexican leaning against the hotel wall to whom the Consul, slapping his stick over his wrist and with something enigmatic in his voice observed: "Buenas tardes, señor" ' [p. 57(97)]. The man with dark glasses is joined shortly by another man, barefooted, with a shade over one eye, to whom the Consul also remarks 'Buenas tardes'. A few minutes later, as Yvonne lingers outside the *abarrotes* into which the Consul disappears momentarily, she sees high on the cliff above them 'a man standing gazing over the valley who from his air of martial intentness might have been Cortez himself' [p. 61(101)]. The man moves, spoiling the illusion, and then seems 'less like Cortez than the poor young man in the dark glasses who'd been leaning against the wall of the Bella Vista'. The man appears to be following the Consul's movements, and is to do so the rest of the day. In ch. 7, as the Consul and Jacques reach the foot of Cortez Palace, they see some children swinging round and round a telegraph pole, encouraged 'by a man also in dark glasses who seemed familiar, and to whom the Consul motioned' [p. 215(255)]. The man in dark glasses appears once more in ch. 9, like the old Tarascan woman, apparently having followed the Consul to the arena at Tomalín. Yvonne, disgusted by the spectacle in the ring, turns aside to see 'standing opposite, below the band, the man in dark glasses who'd been outside the Bella Vista this morning and then later – or had she imagined it? – standing up beside Cortez Palace' [p. 275(315)]. She asks the Consul who the man is, but he pointedly ignores her question.

The man in dark glasses is not the only 'counter-spider'; there are others in the course of the novel. Two of these Jacques has referred to in ch. 1: 'a man lounging on the other side of the

road' who seems to be a peon, and 'a bald boy with earrings
swinging madly on a creaking hammock . . .' [p. 36(76)]. This
'peon' may be the one Yvonne and the Consul encounter on
their walk back from the *Bella Vista*. The 'peon' is gazing
curiously at Jacques's house, his back turned to Yvonne and
the Consul. They pass him; when Yvonne looks back, the peon
has stopped looking at the house and is going into an alleyway.
Hugh sees a 'bald boy, with earrings, sleepily scratching his
stomach and swinging madly on a hammock', as the bus winds
toward Tomalín [p. 243(283)]. Two other possible 'counter-
spiders' are the man with the shade over one eye, mentioned
earlier, who joins the man with dark glasses outside the *Bella
Vista*, and 'an individual resembling a carpenter', who passes
the Consul on one or two occasions.

Besides the old Tarascan woman, there are two other
persons with anti-fascist sympathies who try to help the
Consul. First is the pimp from the *mingitorio* whom the Consul
wrongly suspects of working for the *Unión Militar*. The pimp
clutches the Consul's arm and babbles, 'All dees men [the
fascistas] – nothing for you, or for me! All dees men, son of a
bitch. . . .' [p. 363(403)]. But the pimp is unable to help the
Consul, nor is 'a patriarchal toothless old Mexican with a thin
wiry beard', who has been fiddling 'The Star-Spangled
Banner'. The old fiddler says to the Consul, 'Americano? This
bad place for you. Dees hombres, malos. Cacos. Bad people
here. Brutos. No bueno for anyone [p. 367–8(407)]. The
surreptitious way in which the pimp and the old fiddler try to
help the Consul indicates that they are aware of possible danger
from the *fascistas* and are not anxious to identify themselves
with an antagonistic cause.

A substantial piece of evidence that the Consul actually is
engaged in some kind of espionage or semi-espionage is found
in ch. 7 when he goes to the telephone in Jacques's house. He
takes the telephone book, tries to look up Dr Guzman's
number, finds it, forgets it; then, 'the name Zuzugoitea, then
Sanabria, came starting out of the book at him . . . Zuzugoitea'
[p. 212(252)]. The significance of this seemingly irrelevant
occurrence, the 'random' glimpse of two strange names, does
not become clear until ch. 12. After the Consul has been
'caught' at the dead Indian's horse and impelled back inside

the *Farolito*, 'a tall slim man in well-cut American tweeds with a
hard sombre face and long beautiful hands' appears [p. 356
(396)]. This man, who seems familiar to the Consul, turns out
to be the Chief of Gardens, Fructuoso Sanabria. A second
policeman appears, the Chief of Municipality, who is named
Zuzugoitea. After learning this the Consul thinks:

> And who were these people, really? Chief of what Rostrums, Chief of what
> Municipality, above all, Chief of what Gardens? Surely this silent man in
> tweeds, sinister too, though apparently the only one unarmed in the group,
> wasn't the one responsible for all those little public gardens. Albeit the Consul
> was prompted by a shadowy prescience he already had concerning the
> claimants to these titular pretensions. They were associated in his mind with
> the Inspector General of the State and also, as he had told Hugh, with the
> Unión Militar. Doubtless he'd seen them here before in one of the rooms or at
> the bar. . . .   [p. 359(399)]

The scene at the telephone in Jacques's house indicates that the
Consul has had something more than a 'shadowy prescience'.
He not only knows of these men in connection with fascist
activities in the area, but he knows of them by name.

In addition to the Consul's role as an anti-fascist, there are
two other significant related links in the chain of circumstances
that leads to his death. One of these is tied in with right-wing
reaction to Cárdenas' policies of agrarian reform, which is
exemplified in the fate of the Indian; the other is Hugh's
idealistic leftist persuasion.

In ch. 5, the Consul, after fortifying himself from the bottle of
tequila stashed in his garden, says to his neighbor Mr Quincey,
'I've often wondered whether there isn't more in the old legend
of the Garden of Eden, and so on, than meets the eye . . .
perhaps Adam was the first property-owner and God, the first
agrarian, a kind of Cárdenas, in fact – tee hee! – kicked him out.
Eh?' [p. 137(177)]. Although Cárdenas's plan of land
distribution was for the common good, it antagonised the
property owners who, abetted by fascists, struck back. One
accessible target for the fascist and embittered landholders,
was the messenger of the *Banco de Credito y Ejidal* (as Lowry
designates the institution in the novel) who often delivered
money on horseback to finance the collective effort in remote
villages. Hugh's friend Juan Cerillo is such a messenger, and
evidence indicates that the Indian who dies by the roadside in

ch. 8 is one also. We first see the Indian in ch. 4, as Hugh and
Yvonne are crossing a river on their morning ride. They notice
on the other side a *pulquería*, *La Sepultura*, where 'An Indian sat
with his back against the wall, his broad hat half down over his
face, resting outside in the sunshine. His horse . . . tethered
near him to a tree and . . . the number seven branded on its
rump' [p. 113(153)].

The Indian next appears in ch. 7, as the Consul and Jacques
walk along the base of the Cortez Palace. Opposite the *Banco de
Credito y Ejidal* they turn left up the steep narrow road climbing
to the square, and then must edge into the palace wall:

. . . to let a man on horseback pass, a fine-featured Indian of the poorer class,
dressed in solid white loose clothes. The man was singing gaily to himself. But
he nodded to them courteously as if to thank them. He seemed about to speak,
reining in his little horse – on either side of which chinked two saddle-bags,
and upon whose rump was branded the number seven – to a slow walk beside
them. . . . But the man, riding slightly in front, did not speak and at the top he
suddenly waved his hand and galloped away, singing.   [p. 214(254)]

The important details here are these: the Indian is in the
vicinity of the *Banco de Credito y Ejidal*, from which he probably
has just emerged; his saddlebags 'chink', that is, they hold
money; and he almost speaks – nothing about Jacques suggests
a reason why the Indian would know him; for a number of
reasons he might know the Consul. It is possible that the
Consul's anti-fascist proclivities have involved him, however
tangentially, in the credit financing aspect of Cárdenas'
agrarian reform program. His sympathies seem known to the
Indian and, later, to enemies of the program as well.

Next we find the Indian in ch. 8, lying beside the road. Hugh,
the Consul, the *pelado* from the fascist cantina *El Amor de los
Amores*, and other passengers alight from the bus to investigate.
With the Indian obviously dying, Hugh is anxious to do
something, but the Consul seems lost in reflection. As Hugh
starts to touch the Indian and is stopped by one of the bus
passengers, the Consul says, 'You can't touch him – it's the
law', and Hugh thinks that the Consul looked 'as though he
would like to get as far from this scene as possible . . .'
[p. 245(285)]. The *pelado* whips the Indian's hat off to reveal a
cruel wound on the side of his head and a small pile of money.
Still no one does anything. After a time Hugh and the Consul go

over to inspect the horse. They both recall having seen the horse earlier, and the Consul asks, 'Did you notice if it had any saddle-bags on when you saw it? It had when I think I saw it' [p. 249(289)].

In a moment 'three smiling vigilantes' approach. The Consul anxiously tries to get Hugh back on the bus, pointing out that these are 'not the pukka police anyhow, only those birds [of the *Unión Militar*] I told you about . . .' [p. 250(290)]. The bus moves away with the Consul restraining Hugh, and the Indian, near death, in the hands of the 'vigilantes'.

As the bus nears Tomalín, we discover that the *pelado* has stolen the Indian's small pile of money. He makes no effort to conceal his theft, and, in fact, pays his fare from the loot. Aside from the symbolic significance, the *pelado's* action seems a gesture of fascist defiance against the agrarian policies of the Cárdenas regime. Since the *pelado's* brother is the proprietor of the fascist cantina *El Amor de los Amores*, it is possible that the *pelado* has some knowledge of the scheme which has resulted in the murder of the Indian.

In ch. 10, with the Consul in the toilet of the *Salón Ofélia*, Yvonne and Hugh begin to discuss the death of the Indian. Yvonne says she thinks the Indian was 'just some poor man riding from market who'd taken too much pulque, and fell off his horse, and was being taken care of, but then we arrived, and he was robbed . . .' [p. 298(338)]. But Hugh has begun to see the political implications of the situation, and has surmised that the 'thief is a fascist, though of some ignominious sort, probably a spy on other spies or – '. Then, in response to Yvonne's question, '. . . What *is* the Ejidal, Hugh?', Hugh answers, ' – a bank that advances money to finance collective efforts in the villages . . . These messengers have a dangerous job. . . . Sometimes they travel disguised as, well, peons . . . From something Geoff said . . . Putting two and two together . . . I thought the poor man might have been a bank messenger . . .' [p. 299(339)]. After agreeing that the Indian and horse were the same they saw that morning, Hugh and Yvonne try to settle whether or not the horse had saddle-bags when they saw it. Yvonne says she thinks it did. Then she remembers that there is an Ejidal Bank in Quauhnahuac, near the Cortez Palace, and Hugh asserts, ' – lots of people . . . don't

like the Credit Banks and don't like Cárdenas either, as you
know, or have any use for his agrarian reform laws – '
[p. 299(339)].

The incident of the Indian reappears significantly once more
in the book: the Indian's horse is directly responsible for
Yvonne's death and indirectly responsible for the Consul's
death. From the door of the *Farolito* the Consul's gaze rests on
the horse he earlier has seen led up the path from the forest.
Suddenly he recognises it as the Indian's horse. He goes over
and pats the animal, whose saddle-bags have been restored.
Suddenly the Consul realises:

> ... those saddle-bags no longer chinked. Unbidden, an explanation of this
> afternoon's events came to the Consul. ... It had been those vigillante
> hombres who'd turned up on the road this afternoon, and here, in Parián, as
> he'd told Hugh, was their headquarters. ... those Unión Militar fellows were
> at the bottom, in an insanely complicated manner but still at the bottom, of
> the whole business.   [p. 355(395)]

The Consul's reflections are interrupted by the Chief of
Rostrums who snatches the bridle from his hands. Back inside
the *Farolito*, he faces the accusations of the *fascistas*. Moments
before he is shot, striking out, the Consul charges, 'You killed
that Indian. You tried to kill him and make it look like an
accident. . . . You're all in it. Then more of you came up and
took his horse' [p. 372(412)]. The Consul's last act is to tear the
horse's bridle loose. The three shots that kill him terrify the
horse, making it plunge back down the path into the forest
where, in a few moments, it tramples Yvonne to death.

The relationship of the Indian and what he represents to the
deaths of the Consul and Yvonne should be clear from the
foregoing discussion. But one point remains to be cleared up:
exactly why do members of the *Unión Militar* decide to kill the
Consul? We can go as far back as ch. 6 for information.
Preparatory to the Tomalín trip Hugh is shaving the Consul,
who reads items at random from *El Universal*. The Consul notes
that ' "grave objections" have been made to the immodest
behaviour of certain police chiefs in Quauhnahuac. "Grave
objections to – " what's this – "performing their private
functions in public" – ' [p. 185(225)]. For Hugh's benefit the
Consul says, 'those birds referred to are not police in the strict
sense . . .'. Then, after asking Hugh if he has ever heard of the

Unión Militar, he explains that this organisation is 'affiliated to the Military Police, by which they're covered, so to speak, because the Inspector General, who *is* the Military Police, is a member. So is the Jefe de Jardineros, I believe' [p. 186(226)]. 'In a slightly lowered tone' he adds 'there is this Unión Militar, sinarquistas, whatever they're called, if you're interested, I'm not personally – and their headquarters used to be the policía de Seguridad here, though it isn't any longer, but in Parián somewhere, I heard' [p. 187(227)]. Despite the Consul's disclaimer that he is not interested, the fact that he discusses the matter with Hugh 'in a slightly lowered tone' signifies not only that he is interested, but also that he is not anxious to be overheard. We have seen that members of the *Unión Militar* 'take care' of the dying Indian in ch. 8, then lead his horse back to the *Farolito*. Before the Consul sees the horse he notices members of this 'special police group' crossing the square. 'Con German friends, doubtless', the Consul thinks, referring to the fascist infiltration of the organisation [p. 342(383)].[6]

It is apparent from what happens subsequently in the *Farolito* that the Consul's death is not contrived on the spur of the moment, but that the *fascistas* seize upon a number of pretexts to hasten the death of one detrimental to their interests. The Consul has raised the suspicions of Diosdado, the bartender, by tracing a map of Spain on the bar in a sentimental tribute to Granada, where he and Yvonne met. Then his failure to pay for his drinks or for the whore, and his attention to the Indian's horse, compound the suspicion. The last twenty pages of the novel, after the Consul is forced back inside the *Farolito*, contain a mass of accusation and denial, of confused drunken rhetoric, of wild mixing of past and present in the Consul's mind, with fragments from Yvonne's imploring letters standing as ironic interpolations. Throughout the passage one is aware of the inexorable march of the *Unión Militar's* 'justice'. The Chief of Rostrums asks the Consul, 'You Bolsheviki prick? You member of the Brigade Internationale and stir up trouble?' [p. 357(397)]. The Consul answers firmly no, but his words have no effect. When the Chief of Municipality asks the Consul's name, he answers, 'William Blackstone'. This harmless, whimsical lie, has unfortunate repercussions, because having once asserted that he is Blackstone, the Consul cannot very well say that he was joking, that he is, instead, Geoffrey Firmin, former British Consul to Quauhnahuac. As the Consul for the first time realises the tangibility of his danger, the Chief of Rostrums and Chief of Gardens go behind the bar to make an ominous telephone call, apparently to the Inspector General to get approval for what they plan to do with the Consul.

The Consul remains where he is, as if paralysed, refusing offers of help, refusing to move (for one reason, because he needs a drink for the road). The Chief of Gardens and the Chief of Rostrums return from the telephone, and 'Soon, preposterous things were being said between them again without adequate reason . . .' [p. 369(409)]. Then the Chief of Rostrums plunges his hand into the Consul's jacket pocket and extracts, among other things, the copy of the telegram Hugh had sent early that morning to the London *Globe*.[7] The telegram informs the *Globe*, as Hugh tells Yvonne in ch. 4, that 'The C.T.M. . . . the Confederation of Mexican Workers, have sent a petition. They object to certain Teutonic hugger-mugger in this state' [p. 100(140)]. But the exact contents of the telegram do not matter to the 'Chiefs' – they are interested in isolated words such as '*see tee emma*', '*Londres Press*', '*antisemitic campaign*', '*German behind*', '*jews*' [p. 369(409)]. 'It say you are Juden', the Chief of Rostrums concludes. The fact that the telegram is signed '*Firmin*' contradicts the Consul's earlier claim that he is William Blackstone. Then the final, damning piece of evidence, once again ironically supplied through Hugh: a membership card in the '*Federacion Anarquista Iberica*'. 'You anticrista. Si, you anticrista prik. . . . And Juden', the Chief of Rostrums says, with finality [p. 370(410)].

After the Chief of Gardens tells the Consul he must come to prison, the Consul struggles to free himself. The Chief of Rostrums grows more menacing: 'You are no a de wrider, you are de espider, and we shoota de espiders in Méjico. . . . You Al Capón. You a Jew chingao. . . . You arc a spider' [p. 371(411)]. The Consul tears himself free, strikes out at the 'Chiefs', stumbles outside, and falls over a tussock of grass. The Chief of Rostrums looks down at him, 'We have found out – on the telephone – is it right? – that you are a criminal' [p. 373(413)]. What the 'Chiefs' have confirmed on the telephone is that the Consul is an enemy of the fascists, and that he should be destroyed. 'I blow you wide open from your knees up, you Jew chingao', the Chief of Rostrums warns, and he is as good as his word. Three shots ring out, and the Consul falls. 'Christ', he remarks, flat on his face in the grass, 'this is a dingy way to die' [p. 373(413)].

Thus the last piece has been fitted into the intricate mosaic of doom which Lowry constructs for his protagonist. Each piece is an indispensable part of the whole; the composite of all the pieces seems as indivisible and as inevitable as a great work of art. Indeed, I am tempted to argue that the Consul's passage to his death is the most significant and aesthetically satisfying event in his whole life, which has been a compendium of uncompleted projects, unfulfilled promises and unrealised potential.

SOURCE: section ('A Mosaic of Doom') extracted from '*Under the Volcano*: A Reading of the "Immediate Level"', *Tulane Studies in English*, 16 (1968), pp. 77–91.

NOTES

[Reorganised and renumbered from the original – Ed.]

1. This clash of ideologies is exemplified in the pattern of the Consul's destruction: he is accused of Communist sympathies by the fascist militiamen who murder him.

2. Henry Bamford Parkes, *A History of Mexico* (Boston, Mass., 1950).

3. At one point in Oaxaca, Lowry was thrown in jail by fascist-oriented policemen, ostensibly because of passport difficulties, but, according to Lowry, because of his professed liberal sympathies. See *Selected Letters of Malcolm Lowry*, pp. 11–16.

4. In ch. 5, Yvonne says to Hugh, 'you have to look at everything carefully to be sure there're no spiders' [pp. 144–5(184–5)]. She is talking about the bougainvillaea she is holding in her arms which Hugh is helping her arrange, but his remark might apply to the whole situation in the novel. Knowing Lowry, I would say that the 'spiders' in the bougainvillaea are emblematic of the ubiquitous 'spiders' of the Mexican scene.

5. I do not mean to deny here that the Consul's remaining in Quauhnahuac is partially a result of his grief over Yvonne's departure, and of his alcoholism.

6. The phrase is taken from the comical menu perused by the characters at the *Salón Ofélia* in ch. 10 [pp. 292–3(332–3)].

7. Ironically, after the Consul's pockets have been emptied by his upside-down ride on the 'Máquina Infernal' in ch. 7, a young girl has thoughtfully restored in the telegram to him [p. 226(266)].

Andrew J. Pottinger   The Consul's 'Murder' (1976)

The majority of *Under the Volcano*'s critics have directed their attention away from any interpretation of the work's psychological or 'literal' level, and the consequent emphasis on symbolic and mythic interpretation has seriously dehumanised the novel. Further, the reader who fails to consider in detail this 'immediate' level of *Under the Volcano* may come to overlook a major component of Lowry's meanings – a dimension of irony, centred on the theme of alienation, which he painstakingly and specifically built into the novel during its rewriting, and which emerges only through an alert reading of the work as an 'engaged' novel, an account of human confrontation in historical time.

Lowry adopted a fictional technique in his major novel which conforms, more exactly than interpretations of the novel's mythic structures tend to recognise, to Sartre's description of the modern novelist's imperative:

... we had to people our books with minds that were half lucid and half overcast, some of which we might consider with more sympathy than others, but none of which would have a privileged point of view either upon the event or upon himself. We had to present creatures whose reality would be the tangled and contradictory tissue of each one's *evaluations* of all the other characters – himself included – and the evaluation by all the others of himself, and who could never decide from within whether the changes of their destinies came from their own efforts, from their own faults, or from the course of the universe.

Finally, we had to leave doubts, expectations and the unachieved throughout our works, leaving it up to the reader to conjecture for himself by giving him the feeling, that his view of the plot and the characters was merely one among many others.[1]

Under the Volcano conforms to this prescription by presenting the critical reader with a universe of inter-personal evaluation which parallels in its complexity that of his own day-to-day experience. It is thus as difficult for him to make 'final' *moral* judgments of the actions in Lowry's fictional world as it is to answer the moral questions he actually faces every day.

By way of preliminary illustration, consider an action whose setting is even more politically intense than the Mexico of *Under the Volcano* – Robert Jordan's killing the young Spaniard who opposes his leadership of the guerrilla force in Hemingway's *For Whom the Bell Tolls*. Hemingway goes to great lengths to present all the evidence most readers need in order to exculpate Robert from any moral guilt. The question of moral guilt arises, and is determined conclusively, within the fictional world of the novel; the reader is only called upon to assent, not to deliberate. His reading experience, in this particular respect, is very unlike his experience of day-to-day moral issues where the relevant evidence he might like to have in order to make a decision is not always available, and where other evidence seems intractably ambiguous in its moral implications. Hemingway's fictional world is morally simplified for his reader in a way that Lowry's is not.

Hemingway cannot, of course, be fairly taken as a representative for other modern novelists either in general or in particular. His position is extreme. Other novelists, however, may present far more complex moral worlds than Robert Jordan's while, nevertheless, setting out just as Hemingway does to clarify the issues involved on the reader's behalf. But the extremism of Hemingway's fictional technique in this respect makes his treatment of Robert Jordan's action an especially illuminating contrast with Lowry's treatment of a similar fictional event. Geoffrey Firmin's violent death at the hands of the three 'Chiefs of Police' seems quite clearly to raise the same kind of moral issues as Hemingway 'disposes of' in the case of Robert Jordan – issues which any comprehensive interpretation of the intense final chapter, and hence of *Under the Volcano* as a whole, ought to consider. In fact, a conscientious reading of this last chapter shows that moral guilt for Geoffrey's death is not positively ascribed by Lowry's narrator to anybody in particular, least of all to the men who actually kill him.

Lowry's narrative stance, unlike Hemingway's, forces the critical reader to note, above all, the temporal nature of the protagonist's situation; the 'events' taking place in Parián, at the Farolito, have to be interpreted by each of the participants in the drama before they can act upon them. The same 'fact' *may* be fitted into different patterns in the minds of different

observers and so come to acquire quite divergent significance
for Geoffrey on the one hand and for the three police chiefs who
kill him on the other. Unlike the reader, the three police chiefs
and Geoffrey do not have the luxury of time in which to analyse
each other's actions as objectively as possible; they are not free,
as the reader is, to evaluate the various possible, but equally
plausible interpretations of their adversaries' behaviour.

A comparison of the 'Mexican version' of the novel[2] with the
published one precisely highlights the attention that Lowry
paid during revision to the construction of a pattern of
incriminating circumstantial evidence that mounts up, piece
by piece throughout the final chapter, against the Consul.
Many, if not most, of the changes made by Lowry to this
chapter were features that increased the damning appearance
of Geoffrey's behaviour in the eyes of the three chiefs who must
interpret what they see under the pressures of passing time.
That the Consul omits paying for his drinks and for María is a
modification of Lowry's original plan, as is the presence in
Geoffrey's jacket of Yvonne's letters addressed to 'Firmin', and
Hugh's incriminating documents. In the Mexican version of
the novel the Consul had destroyed the letters by the time he
came to be searched, and he had not lost his passport earlier in
the day. Geoffrey's drawing the map of Spain is similarly an
addition in the later version of this chapter. These changes
achieve two major effects: first, they emphasise, for the reader,
the Consul's entrapment in circumstance; secondly, they serve
to heighten the irony whereby the police-chiefs, in turn, though
in a different sense of the word, are 'entrapped' by their own
propensity to react with the utmost suspicion towards
foreigners.

The reader has, of course, been given a privileged insight into
both Geoffrey's personal history and his mental processes
through eleven preceding chapters during which his mind is the
focus of attention. The three chiefs of police must gain a very
different image of the Consul. If they have no additional
information concerning him than that which they acquire
during this final chapter, their image of Geoffrey is constructed
partly from reports by the patrons and barmen of the Farolito,
who could observe his behaviour from the time he arrived,
partly from their own direct observation of and discussion with
the Consul himself, and is apparently completed by

information received over the telephone from some higher authority.

The possibility that the police-chiefs have an image of the Consul as an arrogant, drunken, alien criminal and spy who might well 'turn dangerous' at any moment – he does, after all, make an assault on the chiefs, brandishing a deadly weapon – constitutes their 'defence' in the eyes of the critical reader who faces the problems of ascribing moral guilt for Geoffrey's death. The police might well see themselves as confronted by a man attempting to cheat their countrymen and representing their ideological enemy, Bolshevism. He resists what might be, in their eyes, a legitimate arrest while showing no signs whatever of acting peacefully; and he is finally shot in fear as much as in anger when he attempts to escape. Careful examination of two passages in particular shows how Lowry's narrator allows this defence to remain consistent with the facts, and thus refrains from endorsing Geoffrey's subjective and suspicious interpretation of the police-chiefs' actions. In the scene leading directly to the shooting, the Consul's killer is described in detail:

The Chief of Rostrums was looking down at him. . . . 'What the hell you think you do around here? You *pelado*, eh? It's no good for your health. I shoot de twenty people.' *It was half a threat, half confidential.* . . .
 'I blow you wide open from your knees up, you Jew *chingao*', *warned* the Chief of Rostrums. . . .   [My emphases]

The language the 'objective' narrator chooses to describe the Consul's killer is reserved and non-committal as far as moral judgment is concerned, and actually tends to intensify the moral ambiguity of the Chief of Rostrums' position. The use of the terms 'threat' and 'warned' suggests that up to this stage there may be no 'premeditation' in the Chief of Rostrums' mind. His behaviour, verbal and otherwise, is quite consistent with his having an image of the Consul as a dangerous criminal. The three chiefs may well have had their image of the Consul confirmed on the telephone, and it is thus ignorance and mistaken identity, combined with suspicion, which lead to their shooting a politically and legally innocent man. Hugh, whose documents Geoffrey is mistakenly carrying, and which incriminate him so clearly in the eyes of the police, is, indeed, many of the things which the police-chiefs suspect Geoffrey of being. He is staying with the Consul for only a few days before sailing to Spain with a cargo of high explosives, and, as a journalist, he is sending information to England which reflects adversely on the *Sinarquista* cause.

The reader might conclude from this that the chiefs are morally justified in *arresting* Geoffrey, but that their warnings and threats are shown to be nothing but camouflage for a more sinister purpose: such harassment would make any man react violently. This, however, would constitute a moral decision on the part of the reader which is not directed in any strict sense by the text. If the reader ascribes moral guilt to the police for their harassment of Geoffrey, he has passed through a *process* of judgment similar to that which he undertakes in the comparable situations of everyday life. He comes to a decision that Geoffrey's lying about his name, carrying incriminating documents, lack of a passport and drunken arrogance is insufficient warrant for the police-chiefs' response; but this decision will be based on the reader's own moral code – not upon any code implied or set forth in the novel. Lowry structures the moral universe of *Under the Volcano* in such a manner that the narrative voice sanctions no particular interpretation or evaluation of its fictional events. The reader is left, as Sartre puts it, 'with doubts, speculations and the unachieved'; and he is left, like the protagonists, 'to bet, to conjecture without evidence, to undertake in uncertainty and persevere without hope'.[3] Without more evidence than Lowry is willing to allow his reader, in the form, for example, of omniscient insight into the police-chiefs' minds, the novel raises the moral issues surrounding a man's violent death and yet, effectively, leaves the reader in little better a position than the protagonists when it comes to resolving them.

This point is further borne out by the narrator's presentation of the mental image (thieves, murderers) that Geoffrey constructs of his 'persecutors', the fascist Unión Militar:

He started. In front of him tied to a small tree he hadn't noticed, though it was right opposite the *cantina* on the other side of the path, stood a horse cropping the lush grass. Something familiar about the beast made him walk over. *Yes – exactly as he thought.* . . . Unbidden, an explanation of this afternoon's events came to the Consul. Hadn't it turned out to be a policeman into which all

those abominations he'd observed a little while since had melted, a policeman
leading a horse in this direction? Why should not that horse be this horse?
[i.e., the dying Indian's in ch. 8; my emphasis]

The narrator makes no claim here to veracity of vision on the
Consul's part. The key phrase introducing Geoffrey's mescal-
driven speculation is an extreme example of semantic
ambiguity – 'Yes – exactly as he thought'. Given the context,
this phrase cannot reasonably be interpreted as an objective
statement on the part of the narrator, 'Yes – it was exactly as
Geoffrey had thought'; the reader must interpret it as the
reported thought in Geoffrey's drugged mind, 'Yes – exactly as
I thought', in which case the description and deduction that
follow are both entirely subjective. In other words, there is no
unambiguous claim made *by the narrator* at this crucial point
concerning the guilt or innocence of the Unión Militar with
respect to the Indian's death. The fact of the horse's presence
with its restored though empty saddle-bags does not make the
Consul's explanation any more acceptable to the impartial
reader than, for example, the possible explanation of the
police-chiefs' treatment of Geoffrey offered above. Their
possession of the horse does not imply that the police have
actually stolen either it, or the money, which incidentally,
nobody has seen any way. Again, however, it should be
emphasised that to say this is not to say that the police-chiefs
are innocent, or to insist that their motivation is such as to
justify the Consul's arrest from a moral point of view. No final
moral judgment is indicated or suggested by these facts alone.

Under the pressures of time, however, Geoffrey must, on the
basis of the limited evidence at his disposal, make exactly the
same kind of prematurely final evaluation of the police-chiefs as
they must, in turn, make of him. He sees the members of the
Unión Militar not as men but as 'fascists'. In the Mexican
version of the novel this interpretation of Geoffrey's was far
more blatant and melodramatic – he says to the police-chiefs in
his final outburst, for example, 'You're pure evil'. In the
published version, this overt political stereotyping is more
restrained but the principle remains the same. As far as the
Consul is concerned, the three men he confronts are not human
beings, 'innocent until proven guilty', but the embodiment of
everything he detests.

The Consul's prime demand during his final outburst is 'Give me those letters back!' For the police-chiefs, Yvonne's letters are material evidence confirming their suspicions as to Geoffrey's being a spy. However, owing to Geoffrey's paranoid interpretation of the police-chief's role in the death of the peasant, he sees their possession of his wife's love-letters as a horrible travesty of cosmic justice: the letters come to represent the possibility of wholehearted human trust and communion; and the police-chiefs seem, consequently, to represent the forces that destroy such communion. He sees them quite literally as the source of alienation and distrust that allows, or forces, men to 'pass by on the other side'.

The mescal the Consul has consumed facilitates the giving body, in a hallucinatory fashion, to these interpretations and deductions. Because he prejudges the police-chiefs in this manner, as the source of alienation and suffering, he also sees in their faces first, 'a hint of M. Laruelle', the thief who robbed him of Yvonne; second, an image of himself as 'the Chief of Gardens again', as the man who had allowed the dying peasant to lie alone, unaccompanied, in the dust; and third, a further image of 'the policeman Hugh had refrained from striking this afternoon' and who, Geoffrey thinks, is directly responsible for the peasant's death.

The irony of this passage is extreme. The Consul recognises the horror of alienated humanity, and indistinctly sees this lying at the root of his own and all men's predicament; but he himself suffers from the same alienation in making such a judgment of the men he faces. In adopting the most 'vicious' explanation possible of the police-chiefs' conduct, the Consul himself fails to escape from the trap of his conditioning: he fails to give the police the consideration as human beings which he feels they withhold from both him and the common people represented by the dying Indian.

The revelation of this ironic dimension through a careful examination of the novel's 'immediate' level in ch. 12 points the way to an enlarged understanding of the theme of communion and alienation itself. In the final chapter, some aspect of the breakdown in human communication is presented on almost every page: by calling for 'Mescal' as the chapter opens, the Consul cuts himself off from normal human perception; his not paying for his drinks arises from a mistrustful misunderstanding between 'A Few Fleas' and himself; and his initially cynical response to Yvonne's letters – 'Had Yvonne been reading the letters of Heloise and Abelard?' – is further evidence of misunderstanding and failure to trust another human being. He jumps to conclusions concerning the possession of the peasant's horse by the Unión Militar, and drunkenly refuses to give the three chiefs his correct name, not trusting them with accurate personal information. By their conversation on the telephone, the police-chiefs seem to confirm the mistaken identity of Geoffrey with the murderer who has 'escaped through seven states'; Geoffrey refuses to trust in the offers of help from the old lady and the fiddler/ potter; while Diosdado seems to interpret his reaching out across the bar as an attempt to strike him. At every stage, suspicion and distrust obscure each participant's vision of his fellow men so that human communion becomes impossible.

At every stage, too, the frontiers of language act to separate the Consul from those around him. The final scene in the bar-room is obviously an image of the complete failure of all human communication as Yvonne's letters are mingled with the stories of the drunken Weber, and with the deserter speaking incoherently of Mozart writing the Bible. And nowhere is this theme of alienation more powerfully dramatised than when the Consul traces the map of Spain in the mescal spilled on the surface of the bar.

No direct report of the Consul's mind is presented during this episode, but the narrative seems to suggest that the map of Spain is drawn in almost automatic response to his thoughts of Yvonne, whose letters Diosdado has just returned to him. He uses the map as illustration for memories of conjugal happiness with Yvonne, and as a means of establishing a human contact with Diosdado: 'These letters you gave me – see? – are from my wife, my *esposa*. ?Claro? This is where we met. In Spain. You recognize it, your old home, you know Andalusia?' His ploy is obviously vain. 'The Elephant's' command of English is too weak for him to follow the Consul's speeding mind as Geoffrey explains the connection between the three of them: Yvonne, Diosdado, and himself.

Communication, and hence communion, is impossible

between them not only, however, because of this language
barrier, but also, perhaps, because Diosdado is suspicious of
the Consul as an American spy even before they speak.
Whatever Geoffrey says to him will be interpreted within this
framework of suspicion, for the existence of which neither
Geoffrey nor Diosdado alone can legitimately be blamed. It is a
framework created by historico-political circumstances, by the
fact that Diosdado, like the cinema proprietor of ch. 1, has had
experience of spies in the past, and knows they bring nothing
but trouble to a man like himself. Diosdado seems to interpret
Geoffrey as making some kind of indeterminate political point,
and it may be due to this that the three Unión Militar men
eventually arrive in the Farolito. The narrative voice never
makes it clear whether Diosdado himself actually calls them,
and they may well have been called by the 'group at the other
end of the bar', whose faces 'turned in the Consul's direction'.
Even if they are not 'called' at all, the map incident forms a
basis for their accusing the Consul of being a 'Bolsheviki
prick'.

On the one hand, then, the Consul unfairly jumps to
conclusions: he interprets the policeman's leading the slain (we
suppose) peasant's horse as incriminating the Unión Militar
and confirming the suspicious picture of them he had painted
for Hugh earlier in the day. He thus fails to give the policemen
the benefit of the doubt. On the other hand, Diosdado, the
other men in the bar and the police-chiefs all seem to fail to give
Geoffrey this same human consideration. Distrust is mutual,
and neither 'side' can see straight or openly for their
conditioning.

The final futile attempt at unconstrained human communion is made by the old fiddler who whispers *'compaññero'*
to the dying Geoffrey, and it may be, though there is no
certainty here either, that the only characters who can see
straight, who are not alienated from their fellow men by
distrust, are the ordinary Mexican people 'of indeterminate
class' whom, significantly, 'the Consul hated to look at'.

The main critical insight achieved by the enquiry
undertaken here is that Lowry's concern with man's alienation
from his fellow man, in a world without moral norms or
community, is embodied in the ambiguous narration itself: the

reader must become aware of and experience this alienation for himself as part of the reading process:

The literary work, at its best . . . provides *moving images* (in both the descriptive and perceptual senses of the phrase), and thus engages the reader, in Sartre's term, as *homme-dans-le-monde*, as man *in situation*, and to demands not dispassionate contemplation nor political or moral activity, but rather dialogue. . . .[4]

The reader of *Under the Volcano* discovers his alienation from the protagonists each time he faces his own human response to their actions – a categorical imperative, for example, that an action like the police-chiefs' killing of the Consul be morally evaluated. He then finds himself in precisely the same kind of morally ambiguous and opaque universe as that of the protagonists when he recognises the sheer lack of 'contact' between himself and the fictional figures he attempts to judge. They are 'closed off' from him. The narrative gives him a personal history of Geoffrey, the victim, which is full of ambiguity, to say the least, no matter how fully his consciousness is explored during the Day of the Dead; and he is alienated from Geoffrey's killers through his having neither omniscient insight into their minds, nor sufficient detailed information concerning their actual behaviour. The reader must eventually experience his own alienation when he finds himself unable to unearth any evidence within the novel to prove beyond a reasonable doubt that when they kill the Consul the members of the Unión Militar act against their consciences. This will seem a ludicrous conclusion only so long as the reader fails to recognise that the Consul's perception, partly due to the alienation induced and symbolised by his mescal drinking, is as distorted as that of his apparent persecutors.

Naturally, Lowry's introduction during revision of this powerful irony on the novel's literary level extensively affected the very important role played by myth and symbol in *Under the Volcano*. This study must largely ignore that dimension of the novel for reasons of space; but one or two relevant points may he made regarding the shift in relationship between the literal and other levels. In the Mexican version of the novel, myth and symbol served the purpose of 'propaganda' – to cast the three police-chiefs, for example, as minions of Mephistopheles, and

very little else. This attempted one-to-one allegorical
relationship between symbolic and political realities inevitably
presented the political and moral dimensions of human
experience in historical time as flat and simplistic. The whole
orientation of the novel consequently shifted during revision
from being a *moralistic* attack on fascism as the source of all evil,
towards emphasising, through irony, the very sin of which the
novelist himself had been guilty in his earlier version:
premature judgment of his fellow man.

Lowry both recognised and rejected the artistic aridity and
invalidity of his own earlier version in which the major
protagonists were little more than counters moved in the
predetermined and conventional pattern of a mythic eternity
where 'life was a forest of symbols'. He confronted the fully
human questions of life in time which were implicit in the story
he wished to tell, relinquished his earlier commitment to the
essentially static universe of myth, and 'restored to the event its
brutal freshness, its ambiguity, its unforseeability'.[5] And these
latter are the very qualities that the reading proposed here
emphasises as characteristic of the published novel's literal
level. The three police-chiefs remain at another level the
minions of Mephistopheles in the story of Faust,[6] but they are
also far more. The story of Faust comes, through Lowry's
revision, to have a more meaningful and powerful bearing on
the condition of modern man when the figures in question are
not solely allegorical, but understandably human. In the
published novel, instead of seeing men as ciphers, and, like
Geoffrey, pointing to the fascists as the source of alienation,
Lowry *dramatises* the tragedy of a world where, under the
pressures of time, it is either possible or inevitable that the
Consul and his killers interpret the facts as they do. He presents
the reader with a *fictional* world of which it is virtually
impossible to decide finally whether its protagonists are any
more capable than human beings of escaping from the
influence of a world-wide atmosphere of distrust and suspicion
that conditions every perception they make.

The relationship between Lowry's Mexican version and the
published novel, when viewed in this perspective, is uncannily
akin to the relationship which René Girard noted between
Camus's *L'Etranger* and *La Chute*.[7] On a certain level, Lowry

must have undergone the same kind of 'existential conversion' as Camus, and perceived that it was an act of literary 'bad faith' to give his narrative-authorial sanction in the earlier version of the novel to Geoffrey's subjective vision of fascist evil. As in *La Chute*, the real question in the published version of *Under the Volcano* is no longer 'who is innocent, who is guilty?' but 'why do we, all of us, have to keep judging and being judged?' In *La Chute* Camus substituted for the Meursault of *L'Etranger* a hero with a different point of view. Lowry, in his published version, performs precisely the same kind of reorientation by 'deserting' and 'incriminating' his hero, denying Geoffrey's subjective vision the sanction of the objective narrator:

Meursault [like both the Consul *and* the Lowry who wrote the Mexican version] viewed evil as something outside himself, a *problem* that concerned the judged [the fascists] alone, whereas Clamence [like both the Lowry of the published version and his reader] knows that he, himself, is involved. Evil is the *mystery* of a pride which, as it condemns others, unwittingly condemns itself. . . . Reciprocity between the I and the Thou asserts itself in the very efforts I make to deny it: 'The sentence which you pass against your fellow men', says Clamence, 'is always flung back into your face where it effects quite a bit of damage.'

The argument presented here may be generalised so as to apply to the whole world of the published novel, and not only to the culminating, extreme moral encounter. Each of the relationships and interactions that the reader observes, both in retrospect and in all their immediacy, *engage* him; and each one 'ultimately invokes [an] exercise of discrimination and existential choice . . .'.[8] In this way the reader brings himself up short against the intractable questions surrounding his own life: the uncertain relationship between freedom and morality, and the 'absurd' imperative of having to judge one's fellow man under the pressure of time, while seriously alienated from him in a world where 'community', in any meaningful sense, is non-existent.

Source: article, 'The Consul's "Murder"', *Canadian Literature*, 67 (Winter 1976), pp. 53–63.

NOTES

1. Jean-Paul Sartre, *What is Literature?*, trans. Bernard Frechtman (New York, 1965), pp. 218–19 (my emphasis).

2. Richard Hauer Costa – in his article '*Pictà, Pelado* and "The Ratification of Death": The Ten-Year Evolvement of Malcolm Lowry's *Volcano*', *J. of Modern Literature*, 2, no. 1 (Sept. 1971), pp. 3–18 – has noted the existence of two principal versions of the novel: the 'Mexican version' completed in Mexico by 1938, and the 'published version' completed in Canada.

3. Sartre, p. 219.

4. William V. Spanos, 'Modern Literary Criticism and the Spatialisation of Time: An Existential Critique', *J. of Aesthetics and Art Criticism*, 29, no. 1 (Fall 1970), p. 100.

5. Sartre, p. 220.

6. See Anthony R. Kilgallin, 'Faust and *Under the Volcano*', *Malcolm Lowry: The Man and His Work* (Vancouver, 1971), pp. 26–37.

7. René Girard, 'Camus's Stranger Retried', *PMLA*, 79 (Dec. 1964), pp. 519–33.

8. Spanos, p. 100.

Barry Wood   'The Strands of Novel, Confession, Anatomy and Romance' (1980)

. . . Almost every sensitive reader of *Under the Volcano* discovers that the book has a paradoxical effect; its power of articulation is so complete that it leaves one, for a time, inarticulate. Witness, for instance . . . John Woodburn, writing in *Saturday Review* (1947): '. . . I said to myself: you are this book's fool, it has stolen you and mastered you by some trickery, and you cannot appraise it tranquilly until it leaves you alone. It has not left me alone. . . .' [See the whole review in Part Two, above – Ed.]

For Woodburn, Malcolm Lowry stood, with James Joyce, head and shoulders above the 'complacent idols' of the time, Hemingway and Wolfe; he was 'a man who can write a prose that is like wine, who can make the English language serve him like a slave'. Of course, not everyone agreed. Writing in the *Yale Review* (June 1947), Orville Prescott described *Under the Volcano* as an 'impressive, difficult, exasperating book', and Malcolm Lowry as 'a student and imitator of Joyce', addicted to symbolism and pedantry, and betraying 'an arrogance of mind which is a variety of literary decadence'. R. W. Flint, discussing the book in the *Kenyon Review* (Summer 1947), noted that the impression of second-handedness was qualified only by 'an occasionally first-rate second-handedness', and described the book as a failure which 'definitely keeps it out of the tradition of Joyce, Lawrence, *Tender is the Night*, or *Nightwood*'. But such negative reactions to the book were relatively short lived, overshadowed by statements of praise appearing in virtually every reviewing outlet in the United States, Canada and Britain.

A decade after the publication of *Volcano*, in his book *Catastrophe and Imagination*, John McCormick saw the book falling within a tradition of 'experimental' novels, a few of which (*Ulysses*, *A la Recherche du Temps Perdu*, *The Sound and the Fury*, *A Passage to India*, *Invisible Man*) might still be read a century from now. In characterising these authors, he wrote:

For all their obvious differences, these writers have in common the ambitiousness essential to greatness, a mastery of structure, an absolute command of prose diction, an awareness of both the lineal and spatial possibilities of fiction, a consciousness of history and politics, while in varying degrees each novel is a novel of ideas.   [p. 66]

The best criticism of *Under the Volcano* needs to do little more than amplify this simple statement.

The story of *Under the Volcano* is deceptively easy to summarise: it is the story of the last day in the life of Geoffrey Firmin, a British Consul in Mexico, a doomed dypsomaniac who is laboring with the grief of a divorce from his wife Yvonne, and the knowledge that his younger brother Hugh, a political anarchist, and Jacques Laruelle, a sometime movie director, have had affairs with his wife. On this final day, all four are brought together in a twelve-hour drama that claims the lives of Geoffrey and Yvonne. To this basic story are added numerous layerings leading to polysemous meaning for the book. Critical readings of the past dozen years or so have noted that the book has not only an 'immediate level' but also dimensions of 'symbolic patterning', 'spatial form', and 'myth'. Linkages have been traced between *Volcano* and *Faust*, Dante's *Inferno*, the Myth of Sisyphus and the travel portions of the *Odyssey*. The

144 BARRY WOOD (1980)

first book-length study of Lowry described *Under the Volcano* as a
'private labyrinth' whose key was the *Cabbala*; and other
critical studies have attempted to sum up the book with
paradoxical phrases like 'tragic joy' and 'infernal paradise'.
Douglas Day attempts to sum up all of these by calling for a
Gestalt reading which will deal with at least five levels of
meaning – the chthonic, the human, the political, the magical,
and the religious – 'all in motion, all interdependent, all
pointing toward the inevitable conclusion'.[1]

This approach to the book through 'levels of meaning' is not
entirely satisfactory even though the peculiar texturing of
Volcano rather invites it. Occasionally it yields particularly
valuable insights – a case in point being Tony Bareham's
treatment of the various meanings of the *barranca*; but Tony
Kilgallin's suggestion of allegorical levels modelled on Dante
seems to constrict the richness of Lowry's symbolic method.[2]
An alternative to this approach, and one virtually absent from
Lowry criticism so far, is the approach through *genre*. E. D.
Hirsch has argued in *Validity in Interpretation* (1967) that 'an
interpreter's preliminary generic conception of a text is
constitutive of everything that he subsequently understands,
and that this remains the case unless and until that generic
conception is altered' [p. 74]. [Wood will argue later in his
book] . . . that Lowry's posthumously published works have
been perceived mainly as failed fiction rather than metafiction,
a relatively new genre; here I would like to note that *Under the
Volcano*, while typically regarded as a novel, is more usefully
studied as a hybrid form of prose fiction of several strands, only
one of which is appropriately labelled 'novel'. Here perhaps
Northrop Frye's 'Theory of Genres' in *Anatomy of Criticism*
(1957) provides the most useful critical insights. Frye argues
that 'when we examine fiction from the point of view of form, we
can see four chief strands binding it together, novel, confession,
anatomy, and romance' [p. 312]. Pure forms of these exist only
rarely; more often these strands are found together, leading to a
possible eleven combinations of two, three, or all four strands.
The assumption that *Under the Volcano* is simply a novel has
never really been questioned even though the book has been
compared repeatedly to such hybrid literary works as *Ulysses*,
the *Inferno* and *Moby Dick*. Once noted, however, it seems

obvious that *Volcano* contains elements of all four strands, with
the anatomy element not only unrecognised but also the most
suggestive.[3]

The term *novel* applied to *Under the Volcano* emphasises
features of the book found in a tradition including Defoe,
Fielding, Austen, Dickens, James and Faulkner as mainstream
examples. Here belongs everything that Douglas Day describes
as the human level, some of what he terms the political level,
both of which Dale Edmonds has analysed exhaustively as the
'immediate' level, the complex relationships of the four
principal characters, including not only the present time of the
story but also the 'weight of the past' which unfolds largely
through interior monologue; the detailed 'salvage operations'
which each of the other three apply ineffectively to save the
Consul from imminent destruction; the tightly constructed
'mosaic of doom' [see Edmond's extract, above – Ed.] which
includes, first, the historically correct political chaos of Mexico
in 1938 and, second, the circumstantial evidence that leads
inevitably to the political murder of the Consul; the remarkable
portrayal of a drunkard's world, shaped not simply by the
distorted perception created by alcohol but more profoundly by
the clearly articulated burden of guilt which the Consul bears;
and, finally, the headlong disintegration of human friendship,
brotherhood and marriage which continues unabated through
the book until finalised by death. There is no absence of solid,
realistic plotting and motivation in the book, nor do other levels
of meaning detract from what we could call situational texture.
One thinks for instance of the juxtaposed conversations in the
Bella Vista Hotel as words drift from behind a partition into the
foreground dialogue between Geoffrey and Yvonne; or the
layering of thought, conversation and print passing through the
Consul's mind as he sits in a stone toilet behind the Salón
Ofélia. Here the situational realism is in the direct line of
descent from the famous seduction of Emma Bovary by
Rodolphe at the height of the Agricultural Fair.

To this novelistic aspect of the book is added a strand of
confession, mediated through the techniques of stream of
consciousness, interior monologue and imagined dialogue –
stimulated in the Consul by his non-stop consumption of
alcohol. The element of confession, of course, suggests

autobiography, and it is possible to discover numerous correlations between Lowry's life and the Consul's. But *Under the Volcano* is, in most respects, so completely projected as an independent work of art that the book has rarely been criticised as disguised autobiography. Indeed, the value of Robert Heilman's early essay on the book [see excerpt in Part Two, above – Ed.] was his recognition of the important link between Lowry as a 'possessed artist' and the Consul as an 'ailing soul', an emphasis which throws the weight of his commentary in the direction of technique rather than personal history. The antecedents of the confession lie in religious autobiography tracing from Augustine through Browne, Bunyan and Edwards; but the form has merged with the novel in the development of fictional autobiography in such mainstream works as *Moll Flanders*, *Great Expectations* and Joyce's *Portrait*. Perhaps the most telling forerunners appear in Poe's *Ligeia* and *William Wilson* where opium and alcohol lead to a powerful species of confessional horror. But added to Poe's use of distorted vision we find in Lowry a Jamesian adaptation of third person narration such as found in confessional tales like *The Beast in the Jungle* and *The Jolly Corner* allowing for Lowry's shifts in viewpoint in each chapter of *Volcano*. At the same time, even the earlier features of religious autobiography are present, especially in the occult, magical elements of the book – the frightening confessional mix of the Consul's guilt with his lapsed magical powers. It is here that we find much of what Day describes as the magical and religious levels of meanings; indeed, it is largely Geoffrey Firmin's sense of personal damnation, revealed through the confessional strand of the book, that prompted Day to call it 'the greatest religious novel of this century' – though it is precisely the word novel that flaws the observation.

Another genre woven into the texture of *Volcano* is the *romance*. Frye places the romance 'intermediate between the novel, which deals with men, and the myth, which deals with gods' [p. 306], a modal placement that points to the features of the book characteristic of romance. The reader is constantly aware that patterns of imagery and action in *Volcano* are re-enactments of patterns from the Bible, or Dante's *Commedia*, or Goethe's *Faust*, so that a mythic quality is woven through the mimetic or novelistic strand of the story. In the Mexican setting we are confronted with a symbolic landscape of plunging *barranca* and towering volcanoes, a version of the cosmos forming the narrative groundplan of Dante's *Commedia*. Lowry clearly intends us to feel the terror of the sheer drop into this hellish abyss as well as the lure of mounting toward the sun. The story occurs along the edge of this infernal pit; at one time or another each of the main characters confronts it; once the Consul nearly stumbles in ('One was, come to that, always stumbling upon the damned thing'); and the Perilous Chapel of his daylong quest, the Farolito, is poised on its edge. The narrative unfolds as a romantic quest, beginning with the possible rebirth at dawn in the *Bella Vista Hotel*, with torturous labyrinthine wanderings through Quauhnahuac, the passages of Laruelle's tower house, the downhill road to Tomalín, the dark woods near the Casino de la Selva; and it ends with the Lighthouse attained at sunset, ironically the time of oncoming night and death. The romantic strand of the book draws together not only aspects of the religious level of meaning suggested by Day but also most of the demonic and archetypal mythology which he describes as part of the chthonic level. The time of the book is the fallen time of history after the expulsion of man from Eden; the mythic time before the fall is projected forward to the New Eden of a distant Northern Paradise (modelled on Dollarton, British Columbia) which Yvonne day-dreams about during the Tomalín bullfight. The book seems to hover between these mythic times, just as it is suspended between the Hell into which the Consul is thrown and the Heaven towards which Yvonne is 'gathered . . . like a flock of diamond birds flying softly and steadily towards Orion'. If all of this sets up a tension with the mimetic qualities of the narrative, it nevertheless reveals the sure hand of the romancer at work.

Frye's fourth category, the *anatomy*, provides perhaps the perspective from which genuinely new critical leverage can be gained, for it deals with precisely those aspects of *Under the Volcano* where dissension is likely to arise. Frye's own remark is revealing: 'It is the anatomy in particular that has baffled critics, and there is hardly any fiction writer deeply influenced by it who has not been accused of disorderly conduct' [p. 313].

If the novel is fundamentally a form of narrative based upon events, the anatomy may be distinguished by its focus upon ideas; in Frye's words, it presents 'a vision of the world in terms of a single intellectual pattern' [p. 310]. In *Volcano* a single idea is presented repeatedly, overwhelmingly, unmistakenly, so that the book could be described as an *anatomy of death*. As a novel, the book recounts events leading to death; as a romance, the book expands into the huge emotional spaces of the tragic quest where human hopes and aspirations are destroyed through the inexorable logic of a mysterious fate; as a confession, the book explores the psychology of self-destruction, the death wish that leads toward a damnation which the Consul clearly sees and apparently could avoid; and as an anatomy, the book unfolds the idea of death as a paradigm of human activity in every area of life.

The details of landscape through the book constitute not so much an exterior world as a pattern of observation, filtered through the minds of the principal characters involved in the drama. The book is framed by Laruelle's recollections [ch. 1] which occur not simply *on* the Day of the Dead (Nov. 2, 1939) but exactly one year after the death of the Consul (1938) and therefore *during* a time of death. Laruelle's vision is, by definition, a view from the nether side of death: a world of driving storm clouds, stony fields, dead trees, an abandoned plough preternaturally silhouetted against the sky – a landscape everywhere suggestive of wilderness and apocalypse. Given Laruelle's profession as a film-maker and his long ambition to record a modern version of the Faustus story, *Under the Volcano* could be regarded as his completed 'film' – a carefully constructed montage of scenes portraying a Faustian tragedy of self-betrayal and damnation. After the framing chapter, the camera moves into the minds of the other three characters, principally the Consul's [chs 3, 5, 7, 10, 12], but with three chapters each for Yvonne [2, 9, 11] and Hugh [1, 6, 8]. It is the obsessed consciousness of the Consul, however, which dominates. Under the influence of alcohol operating as a slow poison, the Consul's reason is seen to disintegrate into the irrationality of 'the therapeutic drink', the delusion of securing a whiskey bottle 'all unobserved', or the twisted ego dance of: 'What right had Yvonne to assume it, assume either that he was not sober now, or that, far worse, in a day or two he *would* be sober?' The world thus comes filtering through the minds of broken lives – a mosaic of muffled gunshots, ruined gardens, spys in dark glasses, startled horses, ominous signs and tomb-like cantinas. As perceptions, as the contents of the mind, the world seen adds up to a portrait of the dying soul. The camera is steadily focused on the 'great battle' of the Consul, the battle 'for the survival of the human consciousness', and thus the book portrays a long day's journey into night, darkness, damnation and death.

Images of death abound: a sandtrap called Hell Bunker; the furnaces of the s.s. 'Samaritan'; the bloody hands of Orlac on a movie poster; a picture of harpies grappling among broken bottles; another of drunkards plunging, florid-faced, belching, into hades; a corpse at the side of the road; a wounded bull, hopelessly entangled, struggling against inevitable disaster; a towering pile of broken glasses and bottles. Across a mind obsessed with death these images break in quick succession; or sometimes they seem to reel through some intermediate space that is neither in the minds of the book nor quite outside – somewhere a swan plunges to earth; somewhere else a butterfly heads out to sea; a huge black ship sweeps into the sunset. All of this imagery – and there is something of this kind every dozen lines or so – constitutes a converging pattern of reference. The unfolding hours of the day turn out to be a multiple exposure to death. Long before the Consul is thrown into the *barranca* we have seen him go through the experience of death, crashing to the ground, losing consciousness, losing the thread. Perhaps the finest image for this is his carnival ride on something called the Infernal Machine: whirled upside down, alone, sickly drunk, everything flying from his pockets, the Consul is left without money, proof of existence, hope of release; thoughts of destruction flood his mind, among them, 'Ex-consul'.

At the heart of this anatomy of death is the death of love: not only has it occurred in the past (leading to the divorce of Yvonne and Geoffrey) but we are privileged to witness the death of love re-enacted. Brotherhood and friendship have been betrayed in adulterous acts of Hugh and Laruelle with Yvonne; children that might have come have been 'drowned. To the accompaniment of the rattling of a thousand douche

bags.' Hope and companionship, escape and peace disintegrate
even as possibilities before our eyes, just as the world
community is disintegrating on the larger political stage. On
the brink of the Second World War Mexico is crawling with
fascists and spies while the rest of the world tumbles toward
oblivion.

The radio came alive with a vengeance; at the Texan station news of a flood
was being delivered with such rapidity one gained the impression the
commentator himself was in danger of drowning. Another narrator in a
higher voice gobbled bankruptcy, disaster, while yet another told of misery
blanketing a threatened capital, people stumbling through debris littering
dark streets, hurrying thousands seeking shelter in bomb-torn darkness. How
well he knew the jargon. Darkness, disaster! How the world fed on it. In the
war to come correspondents would assume un-heard-of-importance,
plunging through flame to feed the public its little gobblets of dehydrated
excrement. A bawling scream abruptly warned of stocks lower, or irregularly
higher, the prices of grain, cotton, metal, munitions. While static rattled on
eternally below – poltergeists of the ether, claqueurs of the idiotic! Hugh
inclined his ear to the pulse of this world beating in that latticed throat, whose
voice was now pretending to be horrified at the very thing by which it proposed
to be engulfed the first moment it could be perfectly certain the engulfing
process would last long enough.

The world, then, is a living hell of daily panic and paranoia,
racing toward self-destruction; and all of this is focused in the
book in the Consul's imminent death, with alcohol for poison,
and pariah dogs to clean up the bones.

Under the Volcano, then, has a double structure. There is, first,
a linear flow of *events* from dawn to death, providing a
progressive, chronological structure characteristic of any
simple narrative. This is counterpointed, but not essentially
modified, in the larger mythic patterning which pulls the
narrative in the direction of romance, thus expanding the
action into the broader dimensions of tragedy. Both sequences
– the mimetic unfolding of the novel and the archetypal
patterning of the romance – are mediated through the
confessional stream of consciousness; and most of the comedy
and irony derives from the self-delusion of romantic grandeur
exuding from the reeling drunk. Second, we find a radiating
pattern of *ideas* flowing out from and back to the anatomical
center of the book: death. These two structures constantly
intersect; indeed, the major achievement of Lowry in this book

is his use of a symbolic method which allows for an expanding system of vertical referencing – woven against the horizontal flow of the narrative through time.

I emphasise *Under the Volcano* in these introductory remarks not because Lowry's later work is unimportant but rather because it cannot be understood apart from this masterpiece. A comprehensive assessment of Lowry's posthumously published writings must necessarily see these writings as products of an event called *Under the Volcano* just as *Walden* is a product of an event called living at Walden Pond. For too long Lowry's later writings have been regarded as failures, a view which often confuses the innovations and experiments of these works with Lowry's chaotic style of life. Moreover, this view tends to undervalue the importance of writing events as if these are not as real for a writer as success or love or failure are for the rest of us. What we find is that Lowry's later works contain multiple reflections and echoes as the creative impulse twists and turns to comprehend itself. . . .

SOURCE: Introduction to *Malcolm Lowry and His Critics* (Ottawa, 1980).

NOTES

[Reorganised and renumbered from the original – Ed.]

1. Douglas Day, *Malcolm Lowry: A Biography* (New York, 1973; London, 1974), p. 326.

2. T. Bareham, 'Paradigms of Hell: Symbolic Patterning in *Under the Volcano*', in B. S. Benedikz (ed.), *On the Novel* (London, 1971); and A. R. Kilgallin, in George Woodcock (ed.), *Malcolm Lowry: The Man and His Work* (Vancouver, 1971), p. 151.

3. Philip Stevick, 'Novel and Anatomy: Notes Toward an Amplification of Frye', *Criticism*, 10 (1968), pp. 153–65, appears to be the first recognition of the theoretical importance of Frye's taxonomy of prose fiction: 'the single most significant and influential event in the criticism of prose fiction in the last twenty years' (p. 153). One of the few applications is Paul McCarthy, 'Elements of Anatomy in Melville's Fiction', *Studies in the Novel*, 6, no. 1 (Spring 1974), pp. 38–61. Some studies by-pass Frye, working (as Frye did) directly from Robert Burton's *Anatomy of Melancholy*: see, for instance, Nathalia Wright, 'Melville and "Old Burton"', with "Bartleby" as an Anatomy of Melancholy', *Tennessee Studies in Literature*, 15 (1970), pp. 1–13. Ronald Binns's long study of *Ultramarine*, 'Lowry's Anatomy of Melancholy', *Canadian Literature*, 64 (Spring 1975), pp. 8–23, is worth noting in this context.

Sherrill Grace   The Luminous Wheel   (1982)

. . . The changes Lowry made in his novel – telescoping chs 4 and 5, and 11 and 12; using character point of view rigorously; recasting ch. 1 within a tight temporal framework symbolised by the backwards revolving, luminous wheel; above all, creating breaks or gaps between chapters – illustrate the direction in which he was moving. All of these changes help to spatialise *Under the Volcano*, to break up traditional temporal narrative sequence, and to force the reader to consider the book reflexively with a view, in Lowry's words, to the 'poetical conception of the whole': *Selected Letters* [p. 59].

So far publishers' reasons for rejecting the 1940 version of *Under the Volcano* are unknown, and only one specific criticism appears to have survived. An unpublished letter to Lowry from his agent Harold Matson (dated 7 October 1940) records some of Martha Foley's remarks: 'It is a very unusual book but one that we feel does not quite emerge from under the burden of the author's preoccupation with what might be described as the Dunn [sic] theory of time.'[1] Lowry agreed, and in a reply to Matson remarked: 'I think on re-reading that Martha Foley's judgement is maybe a just one in part; there *is* too much preoccupation with time, and the pattern does not emerge properly': *Selected Letters* [p. 39].

During the late twenties and thirties, J. W. Dunne's *An Experiment with Time* was in great vogue, and references to Dunne and the law of series occur repeatedly in Lowry's letters and manuscripts. Dunne's book is an attempt to base an epistemology upon the theory that time is serial:

Now, we have seen that if Time passes or grows or accumulates or expends itself or does anything whatsoever except stand rigid and changeless before a Time-fixed observer, there must be another Time which times that activity of, or along, the first Time, and another Time which times that second Time, and so on in an apparent series to infinity.[2]

This time series gives rise to a universe of Chinese boxes, one contained within the other *ad infinitum*, and the observer of this serial universe is also serial. Far from being a passive receptacle, Dunne's observer is capable of psychic penetration into other time levels or, what amounts to the same thing, of transforming himself from Observer A into Observer B and so on.

The implications of such a serial identity are vast. If an individual can move from the smallest time level to a greater encompassing one, then he can perceive the past *and* the future of the first observer as well as of other observers. In this way Dunne believes that he has 'scientifically' accounted for the phenomenon of precognition in dreams and time travel. He goes on to suggest that by being able to penetrate other time levels and foresee, so to speak, the future, the observer can interfere in that future. Even death is overcome, for when a person dies he simply ceases to exist on one time level and passes on to another.

The entire question of Dunne's influence upon *Under the Volcano* is interesting but unanswered. Agreeing with Martha Foley that there was too much concern with serial time in the 1940 version of the novel, Lowry set about to bury this influence deeper in his narrative, but he certainly did not eradicate it. In the 1940 version of ch. 1, Jacques is a serial observer who *becomes* Geoffrey and is thus able to dream the events of the past Day of the Dead, which enables him to observe a larger slice of Geoffrey's time dimension; he can see Geoffrey's past and future with hopes of intervening in that future. However, the chapter is laboured and unconvincing. Although Lowry dropped his original vehicle for precognition in ch. 1, he did not rule out precognition altogether. Geoffrey's hallucination in the final version [ch. 3] is meant to be a glimpse into his own and the peon's future. The newspaper headline 'Es inevitable la muerte del Papa' functions in a similar way. More importantly, Lowry deliberately casts the reader of *Under the Volcano* as a Dunnian serial observer because the reader who has carefully read ch. 1 is aware of the past and the future which chs 2–12 create.

Dunne's concept of serial containment, which underlies his serial universe as well as the serial observer, is most important for the structure of *Under the Volcano*. For example, in ch. 12 of the *Volcano*, the Consul moves from the bar 'into an inner room,

one of the boxes in the Chinese puzzle' [p. 344(384)] of El
Farolito. This principle of containment is fundamental to
Lowry's book, which is itself a kind of Chinese puzzle enclosed
finally in its 'trochal', or wheel-like, form. The condition of
containment, suggested by the Consul's destructive
withdrawal inside his own circumference and by the images of
containment (bars, rooms, gardens, toilets and the bus)
dominating the narrative, is created by all aspects of the text
from its style to its chapter divisions.

At the beginning of this chapter, the importance of structure
in *Under the Volcano* was emphasised, and Lowry's Cape letter
and his manuscript changes help to clarify his purposes as well
as to underline his own awareness of the formal problems
before him. *Under the Volcano* is a book about failure and *acedia*,
and each of the four main levels of the text contributes to this
general theme. Basically, Lowry creates the story, or
'immediate level', as Dale Edmonds calls it, by using a
traditional sequential narrative pattern.[3] The esoteric levels
(fable, allegory and myth), however, operate within another,
opposing pattern.

In his discussion of *Under the Volcano* in the biography,
Douglas Day maintains that nothing is static in the novel.[4]
Certainly little appears 'static' in *Volcano*; everything is
wheeling, reeling and rushing, but this hallucinatory
movement is circular, repetitive and infernal. The gigantic
wheeling form of the book is only one symbol of the paralysis
portrayed on all levels. Time most certainly moves within the
fictional world of twelve consecutive hours in a single day, and
the total time span includes the pasts of the main characters, as
well as glimpses of the future; but the meaning of the text arises
only in part from this sense of what Forster called the 'and then,
and then' of the narrative. Equally important is a reflexive
pattern which, together with the circular form of the novel,
parallels and at points threatens to subsume the sequential
narrative of events. It is this pattern which creates what some
critics describe as 'spatial form', or what Tzvetan Todorov
describes as a 'vertical . . . narrative of substitutions'.[5]

There are, then, two conflicting narrative patterns or
rhythms in *Under the Volcano*, and to understand *Volcano* is, in
large part, to understand how these two function together to

constitute the narrative organisation of the text. On the one hand, Lowry exploits a reader's expectation of sequential temporal flow. The cryptic narrator of the novel is present only as a voice that introduces the reader to Quauhnahuac, comments obliquely upon the story, tells of Geoffrey's burial in the *barranca*, and keeps the tale moving with the consequent illusion of time passing and of one event leading on into another. Geoffrey himself is constantly aware that time is passing. Throughout the hot, tragic day the reader hears a relentless ticking as the characters constantly check the time on ubiquitous Mexican clocks. Horological time – a relentless, mechanised time totally removed from the psychological time of human suffering – represents the civilised, technological world that repels and mocks the Consul. On the other hand, Lowry's handling of chapter, symbol and scene, and the special techniques discussed below counteract this narrative and temporal flow by breaking it up and by drawing the reader's attention away from the sequential story to the symbolic importance of almost ritualistically repeated image, motif and situation. The most significant characteristic of *Under the Volcano*, when compared with the 1940 manuscript, is its spatio-temporal transformation. Lowry went to great lengths to create a reflexive narrative rhythm which would counteract and eventually overwhelm the temporal narrative flow. It is this reflexive rhythm, counteracting the realistic progression of the story, that carries the three symbolic levels of the text. The following discussion is an examination of the ways in which Lowry creates and sustains the double narrative patterns of his novel and the results of these opposing rhythms for the meaning of the text as a whole.

Because the immediate level of story is straightforward and has been so well described by Edmonds [see extract, above – Ed.], it is possible to begin an examination with the symbolism. But in a novel like *Under the Volcano*, which is so rich in symbol and evolving image, it is necessary to isolate key symbols or image patterns. The *barranca* runs through the book linking chs 1 and 12, 1938 and 1939, Geoffrey's garden with the Farolito, Mexico of the Conquest with modern Mexico, even linking 'opposite sides of the Atlantic' [p. 27(67)]. Therefore, in addition to its role as a 'gigantic jakes', the *barranca* represents that sense of inevitable and necessary connection, in time and space, which pervades Lowry's world. Popocatapetl and Ixtaccihautl also have various symbolic meanings, but Popocatapetl functions above all as a magnet at the centre of Geoffrey's circular journey drawing him ever closer. Of lesser importance are the Hell Bunker, the lighthouse (*pharos*, El Farolito), the 'Samaritan', the horse, bull and goat, the scorpions, the vultures, and the numbers. However, the narrative strategy of *Under the Volcano* is best approached through the symbol of the circle or wheel which whirls on forever in the same place. Thus, the great 'luminous wheel' spinning backwards in the dark night [ch. 1] symbolises Buddha's wheel of the law, a cinema wheel, and the wheel of time [Letter to Cape, *Selected Letters*, pp. 70, 80.]. The chapters themselves are like wheels encircling a particular point of view and, as in *Ultramarine*, Lowry employs a protagonist's closed circle of perception, trapped in turn within a self-contained chapter, as an image of the 'madly revolving world'. In fact, not even the reader – or so Lowry hoped – would escape the wheels within wheels of his 'trochal' text because he would be compelled, at the end of ch. 12, to turn back to the beginning.

From the beginning of his work on the novel, Lowry was determined to emphasise the wheel symbol and the related circle imagery. Several passages deleted from the early version of the novel because they were over-explanatory make this clear. For example, in notes for the 1940 typescript of ch. 1, Señor Bustamente explains the reappearance of *Las Manos de Orlac* at his cinema with the remark: 'And neither do we revive them. They return. They redonde, and begin all over again. It is the redonde eternal'. In ch. 8 of the early version, Lowry made the significance of his whirling wheels blatantly clear. Staring at the busy fairground, Geoffrey bitterly reflects:

Round and round went the Mexican children on the improvised merry-go-rounds. . . . Round and round up in the square went the men and the women who tonight would be segregated, drifting round the bandstand when the gutter crawlers would creep in bottom gear around the outer pavements of the plaza, squaring the circle. . . . Round too would go the dancers . . . cavorting like devils or like Dante's trimmers under the wavering flags, skipping all night in the same limited circle, with no variation of tune or step, their homage to St Vitus.

Round and round swung the planets, the moons, the satellites, round and round reeled the drunken, bawdy earth, and round and round went the circumpolar conversations, which were always with oneself.   [1940 version]

Apart from the most obvious wheels in the book – the great ferris wheel brooding over Quauhnahuac and the wheeling stars (in his notes for ch. 11 Lowry jotted down, 'continue the procession of the constellations . . . as a GIGANTIC WHEEL') – each chapter contains its own wheels and circles. The streets of Quauhnahuac [ch. 1] describe 'an eccentric orbit'. There is 'the already spinning flywheel of the presses' [ch. 2]; and the Consul compares his drunken-mystical state 'to the paths and spheres of the Holy Cabbala' [ch. 3]. These paths, and with them gates and doors, are inextricably associated with Lowry's wheels and circles; they symbolise the way in or out of an enclosure, be it a garden, cantina, or even the Cabbala. For example, Geoffrey thinks of intercourse with Yvonne as 'that jewelled gate the desperate neophyte, Yesod-bound, projects for the thousandth time on the heavens to permit passage of his astral body' [p. 94(134)], and the aim of the Cabbalist is to pass through the 'jewelled gate' into *Yesod*, the first sphere (a circle in its beneficient guise) of the innermost sanctum of knowledge. . . .

Geoffrey's vision of the cantina Puerto del Sol during his abortive lovemaking with Yvonne illustrates Lowry's circuitous, deliberately convoluted, style. The stylistic effect is one of immobilisation, what Brian O'Kill calls 'simultaneity', as physical action gives way to the images in Geoffrey's mind and finally to his impotence.[6] It is a long passage, but selections suggest Lowry's intention:

But now, now he wanted to go, passionately he wanted to go, aware that the peace of the cantina was changing to its first fevered preoccupation of the morning . . . now, now he wanted to go, aware that the place was filling with people not at any other time part of the cantina's community at all, people eructating, exploding, committing nuisances, lassoes over their shoulders, aware too of the debris from the night before, the dead matchboxes, lemon peel, cigarettes open like tortillas, the dead packages of them swarming in filth and sputum. Now that the clock over the mirror would say a little past nine . . . now he wanted to go! Ah none but he knew how beautiful it all was, the sunlight, sunlight, sunlight flooding the bar of El Puerto del Sol, flooding the watercress and oranges, or falling in a single golden line as if in the act of conceiving a God, falling like a lance straight into a block of ice –   [pp. 94–5 (134–5)]

Lowry extends and prolongs the moment of Geoffrey's evasion
of reality through the repetition of 'Now', while the
accumulated phrases pile up to form small buttresses between
the Consul's repeated wish for the cantina. The final line of the
passage, 'falling like a lance straight into a block of ice – ' works
in two directions simultaneously. The harsh consonants
coupled with the punctuation move the passage towards an
abrupt close which parallels the Consul's failure; the 'block of
ice' refers back paratactically to the preceding detail of 'the
iceblock dragged in by a brigand with an iron scorpion' [p. 95
(135)]. The entire cantina vision is an example of Geoffrey's
mental habit of circling out and away from a physical
encounter only to be struck by reality as the circle closes. By
withdrawing into himself at this point, he becomes incapable of
entering the one enclosing space which offers salvation – and a
future in the form of a child – his wife's body. The tragic irony of
this failure will be clear in ch. 12 during the last hour of his life.

Even in ch. 4, where the characters *appear* less trapped and
enclosed, ominous images of wheels and circles abound.
Yvonne's once beautiful flowerbed is 'completely, grossly
strangled by a coarse green vine' [p. 102(142)]. Birds loop-the-
loop 'immelmaning at unbelievable speed' [p. 113(153)]. A
stream casts 'mill-wheel-like reflections' on the wall of the
brewery – an image which recurs in ch. 9 – and an innocent
armadillo becomes a symbol of destruction on 'tiny wheels'.
Any doubt about the power of the wheel and circle imagery to
convey Lowry's vision of hell is dispelled by the whirling vortex
of Geoffrey's mind in ch. 5. Enclosed within his garden, the
ruined garden of Eden, surrounded by fences and the *barranca*,
Geoffrey, who feels 'hemmed in', suggests to the Jehovah-like
Quincey that God's curse on Adam may have been to leave him
trapped in Eden 'alone'. Only in the Tlaxcala episode does the
reader again enter so dramatically into the infernal world of
Geoffrey's consciousness. In ch. 6, as 'reflections of vultures a
mile deep wheeled upside down' [p. 155(195)] in the pool,
Hugh circles through his ever-present past until he hears
Geoffrey's call for help. The Consul, it would seem, is suffering
from 'the wheels within wheels' [p. 177(217)] of *delirium tremens*
(if not Ezekiel's wheels). As he shaves the Consul, Hugh recalls
a caricature of himself at Cambridge 'as an immense guitar,

inside which an oddly familiar infant was hiding, curled up, as in a womb' [p. 181(221)] yet another image of regression recalling the conclusion of *Lunar Caustic.*

Ch. 7, on 'the side of the drunken madly revolving world' [p. 198(238)], is the focal point of the wheel and circle imagery because the whirling machinery of the fair is a dramatic counterpart to Geoffrey's 'great wheeling thoughts'. In his panic he boards the 'Máquina Infernal'[7] where 'alone, in a little confession box', he is flung around and around until

All at once, terribly, *the confession boxes had begun to go in reverse*: Oh, the Consul said, oh; for the *sensation of falling* was now as if terribly behind him, unlike anything, beyond experience; certainly this *recessive unwinding* was not like looping-the-loop in a plane, where the movement was quickly over. . . . Everything was falling out of his pockets, was being wrested from him, torn away, a fresh article at each whirling, sickening, plunging, retreating, *unspeakable circuit*, his notecase, pipe, keys, his dark glasses . . . his small change . . . *he was being emptied out, returned* empty, his stick, his passport. . . . What did it matter? Let it go! There was a kind of fierce delight in this final acceptance. Let everything go! *Everything particularly that provided means of ingress or egress*, went bond for, gave meaning or character, or purpose or identity to that frightful bloody nightmare he was forced to carry around with him everywhere upon his back, that went by the name of Geoffrey Firmin.

[pp. 225–6(265–6); italics added]

References to the Tarot, the Karmic Wheel and eternal recurrence cohere to reinforce the horror of this image of the Consul trapped in the steel cage of a 'confession box' and stripped of identity by the recessive whirling. The passage contains echoes from preceding chapters (the looping-the-loop birds of 4, the recessive unwinding of the luminous wheel in 1) and prefigures Geoffrey's 'sensation of falling' in 12. It is at this point that he loses his passport, symbol of his identity, 'means of ingress and egress', and a vital document in Mexico. The entire scene recalls the fair grounds in some of Lowry's favourite German films – *Caligari, Sunrise, Waxworks,* even Robison's *Looping the Loop.* The purpose of these scenes in *Volcano* as in the films, is to create a sense of an inhuman force overwhelming helpless mortals because, on entering the whirling realm of the fairground, man enters another world and surrenders his autonomy if not, indeed, his soul and sanity.

It is not a coincidence that Geoffrey is enclosed in a steel

'confession box' taking 'fierce delight in his destruction', for he
has given in to powers of evil, and his prime sin is his *acedia*. His
destiny is to be so encircled and contained within the whirling
machine of fate that he will be destroyed. Although there is a
type of motion here, the Consul himself is unmoving inside the
blindly whirling box, and time and space have lost all meaning
as the Consul hangs suspended, 'motionless', over the world.
The only further movement he makes during the day is to
substitute (in Todorov's sense) one enclosure for another: the
confession box gives way to the bus, the bus to the circular
arena, the arena to the toilet, and the toilet to the series of
cell-like rooms inside El Farolito. In essence, his situation does
not change.

With the bus ride [ch. 8], Lowry employs his favourite
device for creating movement through time and space which is
simultaneously, for the characters, a psychological and moral
paralysis. Inside the bus the characters sit 'lulled into a state
from which it would be pain to waken' [p. 243(283)], while for
Hugh 'the naked realities of the situation, like the spokes of a
wheel, were blurred in motion toward unreal high events'
[p. 238(278)]. As Yvonne, Hugh and Geoffrey wait for the bull
throwing in ch. 9, the reader is reminded of the containing
shape of the arena by the poor bull's futile circling of the ring.
In a retrospect paralleling Hugh's in ch. 6, Yvonne reviews her
past, envisioning it as a film unwinding mercilessly from the
middle on with the reason for her destiny buried in the past,
perhaps to 'repeat itself in the future' [p. 269(309)]. Even the
bull (symbol of them all, possibly of life itself) resembles 'some
fantastic insect trapped at the centre of a huge vibrating web'
[p. 270(310)]. Ch. 10, the most intensely claustrophobic of all
the chapters, represents one enclosure containing yet another
and another, with Geoffrey enthroned in the centre amidst his
'whirling cerebral chaos' [p. 309(349)].

But circles do not always or necessarily symbolise a negative
state for Lowry's protagonists; therefore, at strategic points in
each of the 'Voyage' novels Lowry uses the circle in its
beneficent form. This is the case in ch. 11 of *Volcano* when,
shortly before her death, Yvonne describes the stars as a
'luminous wheel' rivalling and opposing the 'luminous wheel'
of ch. 1:

And to-night as five thousand years ago they would rise and set. . . . To-night, as ages hence, people would . . . turn in bereaved agony from them, or toward them with love. . . . And the earth itself still turning on its axis and revolving around that sun, the sun revolving around the luminous wheel of this galaxy, the countless unmeasured jewelled wheels of countless unmeasured galaxies turning, turning, majestically, into infinity, into eternity, through all of which all life ran on –   [pp. 322–3(362–3)]

Here the wheel appears in its positive form representing the possibility of hope and salvation through the beauty of nature. For Yvonne, time and space are a continuum: tonight is connected to 'five thousand years ago' and 'ages hence'; life runs on 'into infinity, into eternity'. At her death Yvonne is drawn up, like Faust's Marguerite, towards the 'beneficent Pleiades' through 'eddies of stars scattering aloft with ever wider circlings like rings on water' [p. 337(377)]. The eddies of stars recall the 'Eddies of green and orange birds scattered aloft with ever wider circlings like rings on water' [p. 312(357)] from the opening of the chapter, and these 'ever wider circlings', like Geoffrey's vision of 'infinite evolving and extension of boundaries' [p. 362(402)], express Lowry's concept of the creative aspect of wheels and of containing circles. They are not closed, whirling meaninglessly, but open, forming and reforming, above all expanding in dramatic contrast to Geoffrey, who is at this very moment contracting finally in upon himself. As Lowry told Cape, 'the very end of the chapter [11] has practically stepped outside the bounds of the book altogether': *Selected Letters* [p. 84]. He is referring to the 'ever wider circlings' (a central image in 'Forest Path' and *October Ferry*) through time and space of the voyage that never ends.

The Farolito of ch. 12 is the perfect serial image of the Consul's withdrawal and paralysis, and here Geoffrey waits while 'the clock on the Comisaría de Policía, annular, imperfectly luminous' [p. 353(393)], strikes the note of his approaching doom. The images and symbols of the text fuse here to reinforce the Consul's perception of everything as alive, menacing, and a disjunct projection of himself. Ironically, tragically, for it is now too late, Geoffrey reads Yvonne's lost letter for the first time:

'Oh Geoffrey, how bitterly I regret it now. Why did we postpone it? Is it too late? I want your children, soon, at once, I want them. I want your life filling and stirring me.'   [p. 347(387)]

Yvonne is the one encircling space that offered Geoffrey salvation in a future. There is the space, empty now forever, which he was unable to enter in ch. 3.

The images of paths and gates from earlier chapters which relate the mythical (Cabbala) and allegorical (Garden of Eden) levels of the narrative to the immediate level of Quauhnahuac and Geoffrey's actual forest path to the Farolito reverberate throughout ch. 12 and contribute to the sense of familiarity and inevitability about this place. In other words, the incremental and reflexive force of the circle imagery, with these related images of paths and gates, complements the final moments in the sequential unfolding of events on Geoffrey's last day by emphasising the reader's awareness that this is where he has been from the start. Having lost his passport, his means of ingress and egress, Geoffrey is enclosed on all levels within the infernal cantina. He has lost the Cabbalist's path, he has lost Christ's way of love, he has lost his wife, his future, his life. Doors stand open, but Geoffrey remains immobile.

There are many brilliant scenes throughout the novel in which Lowry pauses in the narration of events in order to suggest the cessation of temporal process through a heightened awareness of space. The description of the burning of Geoffrey's letter [ch. 1], for example, captures the effect of space collapsing enclosed upon itself because the time required for the letter to burn is conveyed in metaphors of space:

The flare lit up the whole cantina with a burst of brilliance in which the figures at the bar ... appeared, for an instant, frozen, a mural.... M. Laruelle set the writhing mass in an ashtray, where beautifully conforming it folded upon itself, a burning castle, collapsed, subsided to a ticking hive through which sparks like tiny red worms crawled and flew, while above a few grey wisps of ashes floated in the thin smoke, a dead husk now, faintly crepitant.   [p. 47(87)]

The dramatic visual quality of this passage – 'burst of brilliance', 'sparks like tiny red worms', 'grey wisps of ashes' – reinforces the emphatically *a*temporal nature of the scene and draws the reader's attention to Lowry's transformation of an evanescent moment into the space of 'a mural' with the 'burning castle' of the letter foregrounded against the *chiaroscuro* of the bar. Of course, the irony of this spatialisation of time is acute because this is the letter Geoffrey never sent, and it parallels those letters in ch. 12 which he had not read – in time. All these letters are objects which never acquired a temporal existence and, therefore, could neither be responded to nor acted upon.

The most graphic example of spatialisation in the *Volcano*, however, is the Tlaxcala scene [ch. 10]. This episode, which Lowry intended as a play or a poster, is a paradigm of the text. The toilet, the 'Cave of the Winds' contained within the Salón Ofélia, surrounds the Consul, who in his desperation wonders why he is 'always more or less, here':

> The Consul sat, fully dressed however, not moving a muscle. Why was he here? Why was he always more or less, here? He would have been glad of a mirror to ask himself that question. But there was no mirror. Nothing but stone. Perhaps there was no time either, in this stone retreat. Perhaps this was the eternity that he'd been making so much fuss about, eternity already, of the Svidrigailov variety, only instead of a bath-house in the country full of spiders, here it turned out to be a stone monastic cell wherein sat – strange! – who but himself? [p. 296(336)]

Significantly, this is the Consul's eternity, and as the scene develops, the sensation of timelessness, created through spatial form, reveals its truly infernal nature: Lowry knew from Bergson that time is needed to keep everything from happening at once.

The scene begins abruptly with Geoffrey's realisation that he is not eating with the others. The toilet of cold grey stone suggests the sacrificial blocks of the Aztecs (mentioned in the Tlaxcala tourist folder).[8] To make matters worse, Cervantes answers the Consul's call for help with offers of a stone, 'A stone, hombre, I bring you a stone' – whether the philosopher's or Sisyphus's stone is not clear. Then Geoffrey, his perception increasingly distorted by mescal, begins to read snatches from the Tlaxcala tourist folder proclaiming the historic importance of this state, home of Mexico's betrayers, with its 'density of 53 inhibitants to the square kilometre' [p. 297(337)]. Key phrases stand out for Geoffrey. Tlaxcala city is *'said to be like Granada, said to be like Granada, Granada'* (the place where Geoffrey and Yvonne first met), and 'in the inside' of the San Francisco Convent 'there is a secret passage, *secret* passage' (a passage which Geoffrey will now never find). The Consul's mutterings about Parián, 'In the Farolito – ', are ironically juxtaposed with another paragraph from the folder entitled: 'SANTUARIO OCOTLÁN IN TLAXCALA' [p. 301(341)].

From the dining room the voices of Hugh and Yvonne, who are discussing the peon, penetrate Geoffrey's consciousness. Together with disjointed snatches of this overheard conversation and disembodied passages from the tourist folder, the Consul hears a babel of voices from earlier in the day – his own, Vigil's, Yvonne's, his familiars', even Weber's:

'Have another bottle of beer . . . Carta Blanca?'
'Moctezuma . . . Dos Equis.'
'Or is it Montezuma?'
'Moctezuma on the bottle.'
'That's all he is now – '

TIZATLÁN

In this town, very near to the Tlaxcala City, are still erected the ruins of the Palace, residence of Senator Xicohtencatl, father of the warrior by the same name. In said ruins could be still appreciated the stone blocks where were offered the sacrifices to their Gods . . . In the same town, a long time ago, were the headquarters of the Tlaxcaltecan warriors . . .

'I'm watching you . . . You can't escape me.'
' – this is not just escaping, I mean, let's start again, really and cleanly.'
'I think I know the place.'
'I can see you.'
' – where are the letters, Geoffrey Firmin, the letters she wrote till her heart broke – '
'But in Newcastle, Delaware, now that's another thing again!'
' – the letters you not only have never answered you didn't you did you didn't you did then where is your reply – '
' – but oh my God, this city – the noise! the chaos! If I could only get out! If I only knew where you could get to!'

OCOTELULCO

In this town near Tlaxcala existed, long back, the Maxixcatzin Palace. In that place, according to tradition took place the baptism of the first Christian Indian.

'It will be like a rebirth.'
'I'm thinking of becoming a Mexican subject, of going to live among the Indians, like William Blackstone.'
'Napoleon's leg twitched.'
' – might have run over you, there must be something wrong, what? No, going to – '
'Guanajuato – the streets – how can you resist the names of the streets – the Street of Kisses – '   [p. 302(342)]

Earlier versions of this scene illustrate Lowry's painstaking efforts to balance the sequence of conversation, folder material and remembered voices as the Consul sinks deeper into his private maelstrom. The disjointed cry, – but oh my God, this city – the noise! the chaos! If I could only get out! If I only knew where you could get to!' first appears in ch. 3 [p. 89(129)] as the Consul prepares for the impending sexual encounter with his wife – an encounter from which he wishes to escape. Ironically, the act of love represents an escape from his abyss of self; it could be his way out of himself. But here in the toilet, as there in Yvonne's room, Geoffrey is trapped. The two enclosures, bedroom and toilet, fuse to emphasise the closed circle of Geoffrey's consciousness. Furthermore, the city of Tlaxcala and the city of New York are like Geoffrey's mind, traitorous and noisy. In this one brief passage, space is condensed and stripped of demarcation or boundary. All places, his house, Yvonne's bedroom, Tlaxcala, New York, exist here in Tomalín, in the stone toilet of the Salón Ofélia, and in the Consul's mind.

Time is similarly compacted in this scene. No distinctions exist between past, present, and future – everything is happening now. The history of the ancient Tlaxcaltecans and the history of the conquest co-exist with November 1938. Yvonne's plea from ch. 9 that 'It will be like a rebirth' melts into Vigil's description of Guanajuato from ch. 5. The present moment – 'Have another bottle of beer . . .' – loses all distinction as it disappears behind the voices of Geoffrey's familiars and the inquiring voice of the English tourist from ch. 3: 'might have run over you, there must be something wrong, what?' The spatial form of this scene with its intense sensation of simultaneity is the perfect dramatic projection of the state of Geoffrey's mind and soul. He has become a self-enclosed destructive circle, unable to distinguish past from present or even to perceive physical and spiritual boundaries. He is in Hell.

Lowry uses some striking metaphors, motifs, descriptions of plastic art, and what are loosely labelled as 'cinematic' devices, to contribute further to the spatial form of the text. Of the many rich metaphors in *Volcano*, the metaphor of the town or city stands out. Images of towns, usually with roads and

communications 'decompuesto', form a crucial metaphoric
network within the narrative and complement descriptions of
real towns such as Cuernavaca, Tlaxcala, Granada, lost cities
such as Atlantis, the biblical city of Babylon, where Belshazzar
beheld (like the Consul) a 'Mene-Tekel-Peres', and Bunyan's
City of Destruction. Most important, Geoffrey compares his
soul to a town:

a picture of his soul as a town appeared once more before him, but this time a
town ravaged and stricken in the black path of his excess . . . then at last to
know the whole town plunged into darkness, where communication is lost,
motion mere obstruction, bombs threaten, ideas stampede –   [pp. 148–9
                                                                    (188–9)]

The novel closes with the image of 'black spouts of villages
catapulted into space, with himself falling through it all!'
[p. 375(415)]. This central metaphor, then, functions in two
important ways. On the one hand, it provides an important
image of Geoffrey's soul which foreshadows his approaching
disintegration and death. The fate of Geoffrey's 'ravaged and
stricken soul', in turn, suggests the fate of all towns, for as
Lowry maintained in his letter to Cape, Geoffrey's fate parallels
'the ultimate fate of mankind'. In this way, the metaphor links
the reader's perception of the fictional character with his
knowledge of experiential reality and fuses the immediate story
level with the political and religious levels of the narrative. On
the other hand, the metaphor functions incrementally within
the text by echoing and recalling references to towns. Each time
the metaphor recurs, new associations develop around those
already present; thus, the town metaphor connects otherwise
disparate scenes and episodes, forcing the reader to read
reflexively and thereby to see the state in which Geoffrey's soul
is.

Before moving on to examine other techniques in the novel,
this is an appropriate point at which to pause briefly and
consider the wider importance of rhetorical figure in *Under the
Volcano*. O'Kill [see Part One above – Ed.] draws a useful
distinction between metaphor and simile and points out that
Lowry uses simile, more often than metaphor, to suggest
analogous relationship instead of identity, but an equally
important distinction should be made between Lowry's use of
metaphor or simile and metonymy.[9] Despite the presence of

such striking similes as that of Geoffrey's 'soul as a town' or
even the controlling analogy of the book – that to live in the
modern world is like living 'under the volcano' – metonymy is
of equal importance to the syntax and structure of the text. In
the passage quoted above from ch. 3, for example, the narrator
presents Geoffrey's thoughts of the cantina metonymically:
people 'eructating', lassoes over shoulders, dead matchboxes,
lemon peel, filth and sputum, the clock, mirror and sunlight,
are all parts of the Puerto del Sol, parts of that special place
where Geoffrey would rather be. Often the sense that the prose
style is weighted down with details results from Lowry's
metonymically organised sentences – Yvonne's memory of the
Acapulco harbour while she scans the Quauhnahuac *zócalo* is
another example.

But the concepts of metaphoric and metonymic association
also provide useful ways to consider the larger units of a
narrative. Commenting upon Roman Jakobson's pioneering
study of metaphor and metonymy, Robert Scholes remarks:

Jakobson finds this distinction between metaphoric and metonymic processes
in language discernible not only on the level of individual expressions in
language but at the level of larger patterns of discourse as well. Thus in any
work of literature the discourse may move from topic to topic according to
relationships of similarity or of contiguity, which is to say according to
metaphorical or metonymic thought processes.[10]

The entire Tlaxcala scene from ch. 10 discussed above is a fine
example of *Volcano*'s narrator working metonymically. The
many voices, snatches of conversation, and passages from the
tourist folder are related to each other in terms of contiguity
and are apparently perceived as parts of a larger whole by
Geoffrey, whose point of view, of course, the reader shares. One
might, in fact, argue that the twelve chapters of the novel are
related to each other according to the principle of contiguity, in
which case, the rich metaphors of *Volcano* would be seen as
operating *within* a larger metonymy. A consequence of this
syntactic and structural strategy (whether entirely conscious
on Lowry's part or not) is the creation of a text in which the
characters, and narrative levels, are contiguous with each other
as parts of a larger whole. While such a perspective on *Volcano*
by no means reduces the power of its specific metaphors, it does
highlight Lowry's ability to create a text which reflects his

belief that events, people, or aspects of an individual psyche (even texts themselves) are not only analogous to each other, but are also parts of one and the same thing.

Lowry's use of motif is, to continue the rhetorical terminology, synechdochal: the Strauss *Allerseelen* stands for Yvonne; the phrase, 'losing the Battle of the Ebro' represents Hugh; while many Promethean, Faustian and other allusions evoke the Consul. Each time a motif appears, it carries associations, regardless of context or chapter. *No se puede vivir sin amar* and *Le gusta este jardín* become more like semantic codes than motifs, however, for they encapsulate and contain the message of the text.

Two motifs which bear upon the temporal scheme of the narrative are the traditional Spanish toast *Salud y pesetas y amor y tiempo para gastarlas* and the Spanish greetings *buenos días – buenas tardes – buenas noches*. In ch. 1, Laruelle and Vigil use part of the toast, 'Salud y pesetas. Y tiempo para gastarlas' [p. 18(58)], but neglect to mention *y amor*. Later [ch. 11], Yvonne and Hugh repeat 'Salud y pesetas' three times [pp. 328–9]. The omission of 'Y tiempo para gastarlas' here becomes significant; there is no longer time for health or wealth – time has run out. The irony of dropping the *y amor* from the toast each time it is used seems clear; the story is about the loss and crippling of love. Important for the narrative structure of the text, however, is the fragmentation and positioning of the toast because its full meaning can only be appreciated in a reflexive reading of the text.

Buenos días and *buenas tardes* or *noches* refer, of course, to the three main divisions of the day – morning, afternoon and evening. At seven in the morning [ch. 2] the Consul greets a Mexican in dark glasses with 'Buenas tardes, señor'. Much to Yvonne's embarrassment, the Consul addresses another ragged man in the same way. Then, lest the joke be overlooked, the two Mexicans nudge each other 'as if to say: "He said 'Buenas tardes', what a card he is!"'' [p. 57(97)]. Later in the morning [ch. 4] Yvonne correctly greets the little girl with the armadillo: 'Buenos días, muchacha' [p. 116(156)]. Finally, in ch. 12, the Consul greets the fascist police with a polite 'Buenas tardes, señores' [p. 369(409)]. The implication is obvious; for the Consul it is always 'tardes' (*tard*, tardy) – it is always too late. The *buenas tardes* motif comments ironically, sadly, upon the Consul's obsession with time and suggests in retrospect that time as movement or change does not exist for him. After his encounter with María, he asks the pimp 'Qué hora?' only to be assured by the filthy little man who is 'fliend Englisman all tine, all tine' that it is 'half past sick by the cock' [p. 353(393)]. Time for Geoffrey is a state, not a process.

In three important instances Lowry uses paintings (murals and the poster 'Los Borrachones') to suggest a stasis that reflects and comments upon the events of his story. In ch. 7, Geoffrey and Jacques Laruelle look at the Rivera frescoes depicting scenes from Mexican history. Time, here the historical time of the Conquest, is spatialised, laid out in the space created by plastic art. At the end of the same chapter, as Geoffrey gulps tequila in the 'Cantina El Bosque', he suddenly perceives the unfinished murals running around the catina walls:

They were precisely the same in every detail. All showed the same sleigh being pursued by the same pack of wolves. The wolves hunted the occupants of the sleigh the entire length of the bar and at intervals right round the room, though neither sleigh nor wolves budged an inch in the process.

[p. 232(272)]

The pictures of movement that do not move, repeated again and again around the room, comment obliquely upon the paralysis in the Consul's life.

'Los Borrachones' adumbrates still more emphatically the unchanging image of Geoffrey's damnation. In ch. 12, as he recalls the picture from Laruelle's bedroom, the Consul realises that it depicts his damnation, with the now forfeited alternative of salvation in tragic juxtaposition. Like the drunkards in the painting, his identity is dispersed, lost, indistinct. The people around him, even 'the ash and sputum on the filthy floor . . . correspond . . . to some fraction of his being' [p. 362(402)]. For Geoffrey, what might be called psychological space, that rudimentary and essential ability to distinguish self from not-self, does not exist. He realises, furthermore, that had he continued to struggle, to act, to break out of the circle of self, he could have become free, separate and distinct like the righteous spirits in the picture. The Consul sees this salvation in terms

crucial to an understanding of *Volcano* and to Lowry's concept
of the voyage that never ends:

Here would have been no devolving through failing unreal voices and forms of
dissolution that became more and more like one voice to a death more dead
than death itself, but an infinite widening, an infinite evolving and extension
of boundaries, in which the spirit was an entity, perfect and whole.   [p. 362
                                                                              (402)]

Here is the secret passage, the lost passport, the philosopher's
stone in Lowry's *magnum mysterium*. By consciously striving the
Consul might have achieved a life of infinitely 'widening',
'evolving', and extending boundaries. The very words, echoing
Frater Achad and Ouspensky, reveal the importance of positive
temporal and spatial movement in Lowry's cosmology.

SOURCE: extract from chapter ('The Luminous Wheel: *Under the Volcano*'),
in *The Voyage That Never Ends* (Vancouver, 1982), pp. 40–54.

NOTES

[Reorganised and renumbered from the original – Ed.]

1. Martha Foley was a reader for Harcourt-Brace, the U.S. publishers.

2. J. W. Dunne, *An Experiment with Time* (London, 1927; 1969 edn), p. 133.

3. In his fine study – '*Under the Volcano*: A Reading of the Immediate Level',
Tulane Studies in English 16 (1968), pp. 63–105 – Edmonds argues that the plot
of the novel functions very well and that events develop quickly and logically,
one from the other. [See excerpt, above – Ed.]

4. Douglas Day, *Malcolm Lowry: A Biography* (New York, 1973; London,
1974), p. 332.

5. The term 'spatial form' was used in the analysis of modern literature by
Joseph Frank in his *The Widening Gyre: Crisis and Mastery in Modern Literature*
(New Brunswick, N.J., 1963). For other discussions of spatial form in Lowry's
novel, see Victor Doyen, 'Elements Towards a Spatial Reading of Malcolm
Lowry's *Under the Volcano*', *English Studies*, 50, no. 1 (1969), pp. 65–74 [see
Doyen's study in this selection – Ed.]; Terence Wright, '*Under the Volcano*: The
Static Art of Malcolm Lowry', *Ariel*, 1, no. 4 (1970), pp. 67–76; Sherrill
Grace, '*Under the Volcano*: Narrative Mode and Technique', *J. of Canadian
Fiction*, 2 (Spring 1973), pp. 56–61; and David Markson – in *Malcolm Lowry's
'Volcano': Myth, Symbol, Meaning* (New York, 1978), p. 9 – argues that the
mythic and symbolic materials of the novel 'assume meaning only when seen
spatially'.

Todorov's discussion of narrative in *The Poetics of Prose*, trans. Richard
Howard (Ithaca, N.Y., 1977), pp. 120–42, is very useful when considering
the narrative structure of the novel. Todorov is analysing medieval 'quest'
literature in his essay, 'The Quest of Narrative', but he points out that other

forms of literature also contain both 'horizontal' and 'vertical' types of organisation:

> There are two different kinds of interest, and also two kinds of narrative. One unfolds on a horizontal line: we want to know what each event provokes, what it *does*. The other represents a series of variations which stack up along a vertical line: what we look for in each event is what it *is*. The first is a narrative of contiguity, the second a narrative of substitutions.   [p. 135]

Todorov's term, horizontal 'narrative of contiguity', corresponds to what I call the sequential, linear narrative of *Volcano*; and his vertical 'narrative of substitutions' corresponds to the reflexive narrative pattern, which is a major component of the novel's spatial form.

6. In his excellent study of style, 'Aspects of Language in *Under the Volcano*', O'Kill relates the verbal organisation of the narrative to the overall construction and coherence of the text. [See his study in Part 1, above – Ed.] He claims that Lowry's characteristic right-branching sentences (the dominant construction in the passage I am discussing) 'mimic a kind of simultaneity', and I would argue that this quality of stylistic simultaneity is yet another factor contributing to the spatial form of the narrative.

7. The 'Máquina Infernal' is a reference to Jean Cocteau's play of the same name (*La Machine infernale*) which Lowry saw in Paris in 1934. Cocteau portrays the Oedipus story in terms of 'une des plus parfaits machines construites par les dieux infernaux pour l'anéantissement mathématique d'un mortel': first French edn (Paris, 1934), p. 15.

8. Lowry, who had read Lewis Spence's *The Myths of Mexico and Peru* (London, 1920), was aware of the ancient Mexican obsession with time. The reason for Aztec ritualistic killing was to propitiate the gods; without human sacrifice, the gods would allow time to stop and the cycles of life would not be renewed. According to Spence (p. 77), the mountain Popocatepetl was sacred to the rain-god Tlaloc to whom regular sacrifices were made. Geoffrey's 'sacrifice' is, then, a small positive sign that life will continue, especially when it is remembered that the Pleiades were considered as the planets of hope (Spence, p. 44) by the ancient Mexicans. On the last day of the fifty-two-year cycle, all Mexicans watched for the culmination of a new cycle. In ch. 1, Jacques refers to the culmination of the Pleiades and, in ch. 11, Yvonne does as the Pleiades rise; the suggestion is that time has been renewed and that the voyage will continue.

9. O'Kill, op. cit., pp. 81–2.

10. Robert Scholes, *Structuralism in Literature* (New Haven, Conn., 1974), p. 20. Jakobson was the first to make such large claims for these rhetorical processes, in his 'The Metaphoric and Metonymic Poles', *Fundamentals of Language* (The Hague, 1956), pp. 76–82; and for this purpose he considers simile and metaphor together because they both operate analogically. In his study of metonymy in Proust – *Figures III* (Paris, 1972), pp. 41–63 – Gérard Genette illustrates the complementary role of metaphor and metonymy in narrative discourse; and David Lodge applies Jakobson's theory brilliantly to twentieth-century fiction in *The Modes of Modern Writing: Metaphor, Metonymy and the Typology of Modern Literature* (Ithaca, N.Y., 1977).

Ronald Binns   Materialism and Magic   (1981)

Malcolm Lowry's *Under the Volcano* (1947) remains one of the most puzzling and difficult of modern novels. The sheer density of historical, geographical, anthropological and literary reference in the novel and the ragged contours of Lowry's career make it difficult to place; critical estimates and interpretations vary wildly.

The original impulse behind the novel was almost certainly autobiographical: Lowry dramatising his miseries as a heavy drinker and an unsuccessful writer, abandoned by his wife in darkest Mexico.[1] Although the writer's biography cannot altogether be discounted when we try to account for the final shape of a narrative almost ten years in the making, the novel succeeds best not as romantic confession but as a modern epic, an elegy to the 1930s expressed through the conflicting lives and values of four *Angst*-ridden expatriates.

In *Under the Volcano* the relationship between the alcoholic protagonist, Geoffrey Firmin, 'the Consul', and his estranged ex-wife, Yvonne, is complicated by the presence of Laruelle, a retired film director, and the Consul's half-brother Hugh, an investigative foreign correspondent. Both men have had affairs with Yvonne. The emotional friction generated when Yvonne returns to Mexico is rendered increasingly dramatic by their accidental involvement in what seems to be the brutal murder of an Indian. In the space of a few hours they are entangled in a chain of events which culminate in a second killing – the Consul's – and Yvonne's death under the hooves of a runaway horse.

The structure of these events and the way in which we interpret them is rendered problematic by Lowry's narrative technique. His literary affiliations were forged in the late 1920s, and his treatment of time and use of interior monologue in the novel have something in common with *Ulysses* (1922), *Mrs Dalloway* (1925) and *The Sound and the Fury* (1929). Indeed, the title of Lowry's masterpiece seems to allude ironically to *Under the Greenwood Tree*, as if to contrast his disjunctive modernist style and turbulent plot with the provinciality of theme and technique which exists in Thomas Hardy's simple account of English rural life. Most of *Under the Volcano* is in the form of a flashback and the bulk of each chapter is presented from inside the mind of one of the four principal characters. The Consul dominates the novel, both dramatically and technically; five chapters out of twelve are seen through his eyes. As in a Conrad novel we first encounter him as a legendary figure, the subject of reminiscence long after the events of his tragedy have been concluded. The Consul's larger-than-life qualities are reinforced by the letter which Laruelle stumbles across on 'the Day of the Dead', the Mexican festival which coincides with the first anniversary of the killing. This letter, six pages of exaggerated purple prose, further promotes the epic status of the Consul. The first chapter of *Under the Volcano*, ostensibly about Laruelle, in effect functions to introduce the reader to the complex sides of the Consul's identity. Geoffrey Firmin was, we learn, an unemployed diplomat, a hopeless drunk, and a man who met a violent death. He may also have been a murderer, a black magician, a war hero and a spy.

The three secondary characters each challenge the Consul's slow suicide through drink and offer alternative ways of life. Laruelle proposes a sensual self-indulgent acceptance of the state of things; Yvonne offers love and a home; Hugh believes in radical social change and the brotherhood of socialism. In turn the Consul rejects them all. He *likes* his solitude, his drinking, his rush towards death. These things cushion him from a world of hypocrisy and betrayal, from the hideous truth of Yvonne's promiscuity. Even Hugh's idealistic political beliefs are, to the Consul, nothing more than a hollow charade, a means whereby failures and cowards sublimate their personality problems.

What seems important in understanding *Under the Volcano* is the way in which Lowry persuades us that the Consul is somehow right to reject these alternatives, that it is *his* vision which is the deepest, the most profound. Laruelle bitterly criticises the Consul for his deviation from normal standards of behaviour [ch. 7]; Yvonne tries to lure the Consul back to married life [ch. 9]; Hugh puts forwards his socialist ideals [ch. 10]. The Consul spurns each of them, and retires once more within himself. When critics consider these moments in the novel they invariably side with the Consul against the other characters.[2] The role played by point-of-view in the novel, however, seems all-important in determining the reader's sympathies, for as Nabokov tartly remarks of a character in *Transparent Things*: 'This Henry Emery Person, our Person's father, might be described as a well-meaning, earnest, dear little man, or as a wretched fraud, depending on the angle of light and the position of the observer.' From the intimacy of the Consul's mind the angle of light does not favour the other characters, and almost half the novel is seen through his eyes.

Although the Consul possesses a vast general knowledge, it is questionable whether he is really a man of erudition of intellect. He knows something of the Cabbala and Swedenborg, and he speaks knowingly of black magic, alchemy and the occult. The wide range of reference made in *Under the Volcano* to crank metaphysicians and obscure learning contributes greatly to what are called its 'transcendental' and 'visionary' qualities; it also gives the novel something in common with other encyclopedic fictions such as *Tristram Shandy*, *Moby Dick*, *Ulysses* and *Ada*. It does not, however, necessarily make the novel's hero a man of wisdom and erudition. It is difficult to accept the Consul as an intellectual in view of his recurring contempt for 'people with ideas' [p. 311(351)].[3] His own knowledge is both obscure and fractured. The Consul is painfully aware that his condition is one in which 'communication is lost . . . ideas stampede' [p. 149(189)]. There is no coherent expression or development of his magical philosophy; allusions to the occult flash up, one after another, then vanish, hinting at some immense significance which is never quite thrown into focus. As the Consul lies dying he suddenly sees himself as 'the pilferer of meaningless muddled ideas out of which his rejection of life had grown' [p. 374(414)].

It is not simply the status and identity of the Consul which remains problematic; interpretation of *Under the Volcano* necessarily comes up against a number of central questions which relate to 'the angle of light and the position of the observer'. Is the novel epic or mock-epic? Should we read it primarily as a realist or a symbolist text? Did Lowry structure his narrative according to an organic master-plan (as he claimed in his lengthy and influential letter to the publisher Jonathan Cape),[4] or is the novel fissured by inconsistencies? It is not only what is happening in the plot which often seems ambiguous, but also what the chain of events culminating in the Consul's death actually adds up to. Lowry went to some trouble to situate his plot against the historical realities of the day – the Spanish civil war; Abyssinia; Fascism; the policies of the Cárdenas government in Mexico. At the same time the novel contains numerous mythic analogies which lend support to a metaphysical interpretation of the Consul's tragedy. Among the most prominent of these are the damnation of Faust, the expulsion of Adam from Eden, the betrayal and crucifixion of Christ, and Dante's journey through the Inferno. Lowry's use of myth has attracted extensive commentary, although Dale Edmonds argues that questions of literary influence and allusion in *Under the Volcano* have been explored at the expense of the problems posed by the narrative on a naturalistic plane.[5] Edmonds suggests that the Indian and the Consul are both victims of political assassination and that myth is of secondary importance in comparison to the plots of contemporary Mexican history. [See extract in Part Three, above – Ed.] This argument is often persuasive, and Lowry himself mockingly echoes the conventional detective novel. The Consul, for example, enters Yvonne's bedroom 'innocently as a man who has committed a murder while dummy at bridge' [p. 86(126)]. Later, in the Farolito, the Consul mysteriously compares his mental confusion to someone who made drunken indiscreet confessions to a barman: '– and why has he told him where he lives, now the police will be able to find out – and why is the barman's name Sherlock? an unforgettable name! – ' [p. 345(385)]. These metaphors, rather like the ironic echo of Hardy in the title, are perhaps introduced to signify the difference between the relatively cosy worlds of, say, Agatha Christie and Conan Doyle, and the brutal historical realities of Mexico in 1938.[6] In a sense *Under the Volcano* is a detective novel, though one that lacks a detective and which evokes a society in which political assassination goes uninvestigated and unpunished.

Under the Volcano begins as a nineteenth-century social novel

might do, by establishing a precise sense of time and place, but
it is scarcely a straightforward realist novel. Lowry retains an
initial distance towards his material: the narrator talks not of
Mexico but of 'the republic', not of 2 November but of the 'Day
of the Dead'. Quauhnahuac, though based on an actual place
(Cuernevaca) is not, like Joyce's Dublin, exact in its
geography. Parián, where the novel ends, is purely imaginary.
Lowry did not trouble to consult the calendar when he set his
novel on 2 November 1938, since that day was actually a
Wednesday, not, as in *Under the Volcano*, a Monday – and in any
case 'the day's background and actions are more characteristic
of a Mexican Sunday (or, possibly, Saturday)'.[7] Other aspects
of the chronology are also contradictory. If the Consul was born
in 1897, could he really have been the commander of a 'Q' ship
in the 1914–18 war?

The more one looks at *Under the Volcano* the more it resists any
attempt to provide a single coherent 'reading'. Ambiguity is
rooted in the very grammar of the narrative. Sometimes
Lowry's sentences are snapped off at the ends, never to be
completed; more frequently they contain words such as
'seemed', 'perhaps', 'apparently'. Uncertainty, hesitation,
ignorance, and doubt are the basic conditions of Lowry's
fictional world. The reader repeatedly encounters problematic
episodes like this:

Once the swing door opened, someone glanced round quickly to satisfy
himself, went out: was that Hugh, Jacques? Whoever it was had seemed to
possess the features of both, alternately. Somebody else entered and, though
the next instant the Consul felt this was not the case, went right through into
the back room, peering round furtively.   [p. 231 (271)]

The technique is reminiscent of Beckett's; authoritative
statements are juxtaposed with cancellations of that authority.
The two mysterious figures may be real; equally they might
almost be projections of the Consul himself. Their quick,
furtive glances imitate Firmin's own guilt-ridden behaviour.
Any sense of an objective reality collapses. Our interpretation
of this episode depends on the way in which we choose to see the
Consul: the cuckolded husband being kept under observation
by his jealous rivals; the anti-fascist being spied on by his
political enemies; the hallucinating visionary, projecting his

anxieties on to the contingent world. It is the narrative technique Roland Barthes calls '*jamming*, acknowledgment of the insolubility of the enigma',[8] and the metaphor is apt, since reading *Under the Volcano* is rather like listening to a radio programme which is subject to constant distortion and interference. The discourse of a narrator providing discrete units of authoritative and unchallenged description is nevertheless present in the novel, and demonstrates that Lowry, while wishing to convey a distinctly modernist sense of dislocation and relativism, was unwilling to renounce a naturalistic framework.

At the end of *Under the Volcano* the Consul dies, but a question remains, of the sort we encounter at a comic moment in *Henry IV, Part One*:

GLENDOWER: I can call spirits from the vasty deep.
HOTSPUR: Why, so can I, or so can any men;
            But will they come when you do call for them?

Is the Consul really a black magician? Does civilisation collapse into another world war, cursed by a modern Faustus? In his heart the Consul cries out, '"Destroy the world!"' [p. 291(331)], and his curse comes true. Lowry explicitly links his hero's doom to the world's: the 'black spouts of villages catapulted into space' [p. 375(415)], which the Consul sees as he dies, may be the bombed villages of Spain, but 'the inconceivable pandemonium of a million tanks . . . the blazing of ten million burning bodies' [ibid.] is a prophetic vision of the future world war. The end of the novel seems to validate Geoffrey Firmin's earlier intimation that his own destiny is mysteriously associated with that of civilisation itself: 'who would ever have believed that some obscure man, sitting at the centre of the world in a bathroom, say, thinking solitary miserable thoughts, was authorising their doom' [p. 149(189)]. The Consul's *Weltanschauung* is magical and opposed to rational modes of analysing history; his interests are metaphysical, his conversations full of reference to the Atlantis legend, demons, black magic, the Cabbala. Only Hugh, the communist, offers a challenge to the Consul's muddled mysticism. When Hugh moves to the forefront of the narrative the reader's attention is drawn to a wealth of contemporary political events: the Indian

struggle for independence, the Japanese invasion of China, the
Munich agreement, and, most of all, the Spanish civil war, in
its closing stages by November 1938. Hugh is particularly
preoccupied by the Battle of the Ebro, the last, disastrous
Loyalist offensive (begun in July 1938 and lost by 16
November). He also recalls key moments in the war: the battle
of Madrid (November 1936), and the great Loyalist victory at
Brihuega in March 1937.

   Judged by Hugh's values the other three principal characters
are compromised figures. Laruelle is a playboy gone to seed,
the collector of stone idols and a Mexican mistress, 'a
confirmedly promiscuous bachelor, with a rather unctuous
possessive manner towards women' [p. 14(54)]. The Consul
plays the stock-market and is involved in some sort of dubious
and illegal property ownership. Yvonne is a capitalist's
daughter, brought up by a wealthy uncle with financial
interests in South America. The self-centred lives of these three
are in sharp contrast to Hugh's. Yet Hugh ultimately offers
only an ineffectual challenge to the Consul. He is a comic
figure; despite all his talk of commitment, the only time we see
him holding a rifle is when he shoots wooden ducks at the fair.
Hugh may be 'a professional indoor Marxman' [p. 14(54)], but
his socialism is, to adopt Engels's distinction, 'utopian' rather
than 'scientific'. When Hugh defends his political philosophy
he refers not to Marx but to Matthew Arnold. His attitude to
the Spanish civil war seems ambivalent. He is contemptuous of
those who depart in disillusion 'to discredit the whole thing' but
describes the role of volunteers as no more than that of 'a
communist fence' [p. 106(146)]. His knowledge of history and
of contemporary events is sometimes defective.[9]

   The lost short story of 1936 and the 40,000-word novella
which Lowry had completed by May 1937 must clearly have
lacked the dense historical reference of the final text of *Under the
Volcano*, if only because many of the events mentioned in the
novel had not yet happened. By shifting his time scale to
1938–39 and situating the death of the Consul against a world
on the brink of war, Lowry vastly increased the prophetic
impact of his tragedy. When the Consul angrily denounces
Hugh's left-wing politics, he shouts: 'Not long ago it was poor
little defenceless Ethiopia. Before that, poor little defenceless

Flanders. To say nothing of course of the poor little defenceless Belgian Congo. And tomorrow it will be poor little defenceless Latvia. Or Finland. Or Piddledeedee. Or even Russia' [p. 311(351)]. As a cry of rage made on 2 November 1938 this is historically accurate. A year later Latvia reluctantly agreed to a Soviet military occupation. Finland declined a similar fate and was invaded on 30 November 1939. In June 1941 the USSR was in turn invaded, by Germany. The Consul, often apparently only a self-deluding drunk, actually possesses a clairvoyant insight into the future.

Contingent reality itself seems to endorse the Consul's intuition of mysterious occult connexions at the heart of things. Lowry's Mexico emerges as a sinister, magical world of uncanny symmetries. The role of the pariah dogs as Faustian familiars or demons is underlined by puns: 'the pariah dog . . . appeared familiarly at heel' [p. 70(110)]; 'It was a pariah dog and disturbingly familiar' [p. 131(171)]. Often the reader's attention is nudged by hints of what is going to happen in the future. In ch. 5 we are told that the Consul momentarily resembles 'a man who does not know he has been shot from behind' [p. 130(170)], and the simile prefigures what will indeed happen.

As Lowry revised and rewrote *Under the Volcano* he crammed the narrative with images of decay and ruin which conjure up a pervasive atmosphere of entropy (Oswald Spengler's *Decline of the West* was one of the novelist's sources). The Consul's belief in a world of magical symmetries and occult causation accorded well with Lowry's technical revisions of the manuscript, since the novelist was seeking 'to make a noise like music'[10] rather than to achieve a credible realism. Lowry gave an example of his 'musical' technique to Jonathan Cape: 'M. Laruelle burns the Consul's letter [at the end of ch 1], the act of which is poetically balanced by the flight of vultures ("like burnt papers floating from a fire") at the end of II, and also by the burning of the Consul's MSS in Yvonne's dying dream in XI'.[11] Such 'poetic balancing' may make the reader feel that the novel is highly wrought, but equally it lends credence to the Consul's perception of an irrational, magical world, since the narrative itself proceeds analogically. Lowry's rambling attempts to explain to Cape that his dissonant, fissured text made sense in

terms of multiple levels of meaning meshed together in a
fully-organised 'organic' structure are not very convincing.[12]
Indeed, Lowry himself contradicted his elaborate defence of
'the foundations of the book, the basic structure'[13] by tacitly
accepting the idea of cuts in some parts of the novel. By 1949 the
novelist was willing to allow his editor to abridge the novel, and
as late as 1957 Lowry was prepared to concede 'some fairly big
cuts' for a paperback edition.[14]

The palimpsest qualities of *Under the Volcano* seem to derive
from crucial changes in the author's sensibility during the ten
years in which the novel was written. In 1934 Lowry married
Jan Gabrial, a young left-wing Jewish American who was
possibly in the Communist Party and who almost certainly
encouraged the social awareness evidenced by the novelist's
mid-1930s work. His story 'Economic Conference, 1934'
(1934), for example, refers to capitalism, strikes, fascist
dictatorship, the Polish corridor and numerous other
contemporary matters. When Lowry and Jan Gabrial went to
Mexico in 1936, that country was entering a turbulent phase
under President Cárdenas, but unlike two other visitors from
that period, Graham Greene and Evelyn Waugh, Lowry was
sympathetic to the President's programme of socialist
reconstruction.[15] Indeed, while in Mexico Lowry struck up an
important friendship with an Indian whom he referred to
variously as Juan Fernando Marquez and Fernando Atonalzin.
Marquez/Atonalzin apparently held strong left-wing views
and was a firm supporter of the Mexican Revolution; Lowry
wrote him into *Under the Volcano* in the figure of Juan Cerillo, a
committed revolutionary socialist. When the American writer
Conrad Aiken visited Lowry in Mexico he discovered that his
old protégé 'had drifted pretty far, politically, towards
something like communism. He had been through something
like a social conversion, and clearly felt a need for some sort of
fraternal joining and belonging.'[16]

If Lowry began writing *Under the Volcano* sharing the politics
of Hugh Firmin (in 1950 he recalled that the work 'started off'
as a political parable),[17] he nevertheless completed it feeling
very much more sympathetic to the Consul's irrational magical
beliefs. After Jan Gabrial left Lowry in 1937, her political and
literary influence on him seems to have faded rapidly,

compounded perhaps by the Moscow show trials and the 1939 Nazi–Soviet pact, which evoked increasing disillusion on the Left. It is worth recalling, too, that unlike many progressive 'thirties intellectuals Lowry had actually experienced the rigours of a working man's life, and what he saw did not encourage him to glorify the proletariat: 'This was not the heroic working class where men love, looking to the future, but petty squabbles, jealousies . . .'.[18] Perhaps Lowry's affiliation with communism had been only skin deep, a matter of fashion. It is difficult to believe that Lowry ever read any Marx, and in one of his stories, 'Enter One in Sumptuous Armour', he makes the odd but perhaps revealing error of claiming that *Das Kapital* was written in Liverpool.

Lowry's sensibility underwent a dramatic transformation after Jan Gabrial's departure from his life. During the period 1942–44, when he worked on the final drafts of *Under the Volcano*, he became increasingly fascinated by the occult, 'taking astral journeys to Venus, casting sticks about in the manner prescribed by the *I Ching*, practicing Yoga exercises, and climbing about in the Sephirotic Tree'.[19] The Consul, initially based on Conrad Aiken, whom Lowry had broken with and denounced as 'pro-fascist',[20] began to engage his imagination and sympathies very much more deeply than before. The text which Lowry finally arrived at establishes an underlying complicity between the narrator and the Consul (significantly the style of Firmin's letter in ch. 1 is identical with the overall style of the novel itself). Lowry's cavalier attitude to his characters ('The truth is that the character drawing is not only weak but virtually non-existent . . . the four main characters being intended, in one of the book's meanings, to be aspects of the same man') is an exaggeration, but it is true that the language and values of Hugh, Yvonne and Laruelle tend to express, surreptitiously, the Consul's. Hugh, for example, apostrophises Yvonne as the typical American female:

Women of medium height, slenderly built, mostly divorced, passionate but envious of the male – angel to him as he is bright or dark, yet unconscious destructive succubus of his ambitions – American women, with that rather graceful swift way of walking, with the clean scrubbed turned faces of children, the skin finely textured with a satin sheen, their hair clean and shining as though just washed, and looking like that, but carelessly done, the

slim brown hands that do not rock the cradle, the slender feet – how many
centuries of oppression have produced them?   [p. 191(231)]

This is an extraordinary passage which goes to the heart of the
mixture of loathing and attraction which characterises the
narrator's presentation of Yvonne. Though Lowry tacks on a
political motive for Hugh's spasm of dislike for what Yvonne
represents, it seems clear that what really repels him is her
ruthless sexuality. The composite woman Yvonne represents is
a curious mixture of experience ('passionate . . . divorced') and
childlike innocence, as beautiful and smartly dressed as a
model, but with revealingly 'brown' skin. In various ways she is
a threatening figure. She has an indiscriminate sexual appetite;
she couples with men who are 'bright or dark' in both a
symbolic and literal sense – Yvonne has slept both with the
swarthy lecherous Laruelle and the younger less-experienced
Hugh. She spurns the claims of the nuclear family, since her
hands will never 'rock the cradle'. She is also 'envious' of men,
although why this should be so is not made clear, especially
since the ways in which she destroys their ambitions are
'unconscious', and the nature of those ambitions remains
unspecified. It is almost as if Lowry intended his heroine to
appear as another Nicole, destroying a promising career as
Dick Diver's is destroyed in Scott Fitzgerald's *Tender is the Night*,
but the critique of Yvonne remains rhetorical. She can scarcely
be accused of having destroyed any profound ambitions on her
husband's part, since at the age of forty he is merely British
consul in an insignificant Mexican town, with vague notions of
one day finishing his book on Atlantis and 'Secret Knowledge'.
When the Consul dies it is hard to feel that a man with a
brilliant future has ben prematurely torn from us. Nor, for that
matter, can Laruelle's failure as a film director be blamed on
her. Hugh's own career in journalism, apparently successful,
has not in any way been affected by his liaison with Yvonne.

The criticism lacks foundation, and is doubly curious coming
from Hugh, who, unlike the furious and disgusted Consul,
knows nothing of her affair with Laruelle. Odd, too, is Hugh's
particularly virulent branding of her as a 'destructive
succubus'. This again highlights the sexual aspect of his
hostility (since a succubus is a female demon supposed to have

sexual intercourse with sleeping men), but the term is a strange one for him to use and belongs much more with the Consul's occult vocabulary. Yvonne is the source of three other violent outbursts of sexual disgust in the novel, and each comes from the Consul: his reaction to the sight of Laruelle nude [p. 210(250)]; his description of Cliff's lovemaking as 'a kind of dysentry' [p. 265(305)]; his Shakespearean jeers at Hugh and Yvonne's 'romantic predicament' [p. 315(355)]. The only criticism of Yvonne which Hugh makes and which seems in keeping with his character is his subsequent comment on her indifference to the imminent victory of Franco in the Spanish civil war.

The passage in fact seems inconsistent with all the other things we learn about Hugh. He seems quite free of sexual neuroses. He is unaware that Laruelle replaced him in Yvonne's affections. There seems to be no reason (in the light of his 'progressive' left-wing views) why he should be at all concerned about Yvonne's indifference to the bourgeois goal of settling down and raising a family. Lowry seems to have indulged in ventriloquism at this moment in the novel, making Hugh express an attitude which more properly belongs to the Consul.

This is not to say that Hugh Firmin is a wooden, one-dimensional character, a target for the writer's animus in a way that other fictional leftists are, like McKisco in *Tender is the Night* (1934) or Peter Slavek in Arthur Koestler's *Arrival and Departure* (1943). Lowry nevertheless loads the dice against Hugh, and it is Hugh who represents the most sustained challenge to the Consul's introspection. A true dialectical materialist would not, one assumes, lapse into dreamy moments of neo-Platonic reverie of the kind which Hugh indulges in when he thinks that 'far above was perhaps another sea, where the soul ploughed its high invisible wake' [p. 167(207)]. The structure of the novel itself endorses the Consul's belief in historical cycles, as opposed to Hugh's linear materialist philosophy. Ch. 1 mysteriously reincarnates figures and situations from the main body of the novel, which is located one year earlier in time. This chapter also shows Laruelle's scepticism severely shaken by a series of mysterious coincidences which seem to attest to supernatural forces at work.

Lowry's evident indifference to society in the fiction he wrote after *Under the Volcano* was accompanied by a revealing switch away from a concern with several characters' inner lives to a single point of view. With the very limited exception of Jacqueline in Lowry's last novel, *October Ferry to Gabriola*, no one ever steps forward again as Hugh and Laruelle do to challenge the values and beliefs of the hero. This technical innovation was accompanied by an increasingly apocalyptic view of history on Lowry's part. In *Dark as the Grave Wherein My Friend is Laid*, Lowry's next novel after *Under the Volcano*, the relics left by vanished civilisations are disturbingly sombre: 'A skull, bored by syphilis germs, had survived: the oddity and the meaninglessness of it.' In Lowry's 1950s story 'Present Estate of Pompeii', the protagonist echoes the Consul, asking if historians 'really said anything new' in the face of recurring cycles of decay and social collapse. History is portrayed as being quite simply meaningless: 'St. Malo was wiped out, Naples defaced, but a cock in the street outside an antique Pompeiian brothel survived.' Faced by such stark and absurd images of the futility of human progress, Lowry's later heroes retreat into a comforting solipsism.

In *Under the Volcano* solipsism, embodied most profoundly by the Consul, is subjected to attack, criticism, irony. The true alternative to the Consul's introspection is perhaps ultimately represented not by the flawed Hugh but by the fleeting figure of Juan Cerillo, the committed revolutionary socialist who represents a genuine 'adventure in a human cause' [p. 111(151)]. In view of the way Lowry tilts the novel in the Consul's favour it's perhaps significant that Cerillo is barely permitted to pose much of a threat to Geoffrey Firmin's inward-looking values. Cerillo, an authentic revolutionary, is displaced from the central action of the novel and remains off-stage, a brief fragmentary figure in Hugh's memory. On 5 March 1949 Lowry wrote to Albert Erskine suggesting that *Under the Volcano* might be cut in various ways, and including the recommendation to keep '[Chapter] IV intact, though we might cut Juan Cerillo altogether'.[21] By 1949, however, Lowry was well on the way to convincing himself that a single point of view was acceptable as a foundation for the rest of his life's work. If he had lost his fascination with politics, history and society so too had he lost what he once identified as 'the historian's willingness to see the drama of both sides'.[22]

SOURCE: article, 'Materialism and Magic in *Under the Volcano*, in *Critical Quarterly*, 23 (1981), pp. 21–33.

NOTES

1. The earliest drafts of *Under the Volcano* have been lost. The much-anthologised short story of the same title is not, as is frequently claimed, the original narrative from which the novel grew, but simply a post-1940 draft of ch. 8.

2. T. Bareham's description of the Consul as 'infinitely the most sensitive and intelligent person in the book' is a typical one. See 'Paradigms of Hell: Symbolic Patterning in *Under the Volcano*', in B. S. Benedikz (ed.), *On the Novel* (London 1971), p. 115. See also the unfavourable treatment which Laruelle and Hugh receive in two of the best books on Lowry: Richard Hauer Costa, *Malcolm Lowry* (New York, 1972) and David Markson, *Malcolm Lowry's Volcano* (New York, 1978).

3. [Ed.] All references are to the Penguin 'Modern Classics' edition (1962), supplemented by pagination of the 1985 Penguin.

4. See Harvey Breit and Margerie Bonner Lowry (eds), *Selected Letters of Malcolm Lowry* (New York, 1965), pp. 57–88.

5. See Dale Edmonds, '*Under the Volcano*: a reading of the "immediate level"', *Tulane Studies in English*, 16 (1968), pp. 63–105.

6. In *Malcolm Lowry, a Biography* (New York, 1973), Douglas Day mentions that one of Lowry's schoolboy stories was 'a parody of sophisticated crime fiction' (p. 81).

7. Edmonds, op. cit., p. 65.

8. Roland Barthes, *S/Z* (London, 1975), p. 210.

9. For example, Hugh's self-identification with General Winfield Scott in ch. 4 is ironically inappropriate. See Larry Clipper, 'Hugh Firmin as General Winfield Scott: A Note', in *Malcolm Lowry Newsletter*, 4 (Spring 1979), pp. 10–11. Hugh also states that the International Brigades were evacuated 'five weeks ago, on the twenty-eighth of September to be precise – two days before Chamberlain went to Godesburg and neatly crimped the Ebro offensive' [p. 106(146)]. In fact Chamberlain flew to Godesburg on 22 Sept. 1938, not, as Hugh implies, 30 Sept. Nor were the International Brigades withdrawn swiftly on a precise date. The Brigades last saw action on 22 Sept., but repatriation was a slow business. A great farewell parade was held in Barcelona on 15 Nov. – almost two weeks after Lowry's Day of the Dead. It is also very debatable whether Chamberlain's diplomatic manoevrings over the fate of central Europe can be held to have significantly interfered with the final course of events in Spain.

10. *Selected Letters of Malcolm Lowry*, p. 200.   11. Ibid., p. 70.

12. The publisher's reader's sceptical response to Lowry's analysis of *Under the Volcano* is quoted in Michael S. Howard, *Jonathan Cape, Publisher* (London, 1971).

13. *Selected Letters*, pp. 58–9.

14. Unpublished letter to David Markson (22 Feb. 1957).

15. Green's account of his 1938 visit, *The Lawless Roads* (London, 1939) is propagandistic and hostile to the Cárdenas government, as is Waugh's more strident *Robbery Under Law: the Mexican Object Lesson* (London, 1939).

16. Conrad Aiken, *Ushant: an Essay* (New York, 1952), p. 351.

17. *Selected Letters*, p. 199.

18. Earle Birney (ed.), *Selected Poems of Malcolm Lowry* (San Francisco, 1962), p. 21.

19. Day, op. cit., p. 295.

20. Unpublished letter to John Davenport (31 Aug. 1937). Aiken later claimed that the quarrel between the Consul and Hugh was a verbatim transcription of a row over politics he once had with Lowry; see *Times Literary Supplement* (16 Feb. 1967), p. 127.

21. Part of the letter is quoted in Douglas Day, 'Malcolm Lowry: Letters to an Editor', *Shenandoah* (Spring 1964), 15, no. 3, p. 8.

22. *Selected Letters*, p. 146.

SELECT BIBLIOGRAPHY

The material listed below is not included, or excerpted from, in the Casebook selection. For publication details of books and articles reproduced there, see the Source entry at the conclusion of each item in the selection.

EDITIONS OF THE NOVEL (in English)

Reynal and Hitchcock (New York, 1947);
Cape (London, 1947);
Vintage-Random House (New York, 1958);
Penguin, 'Modern Classics' (Harmondsworth, 1962);
Lippincott (New York, 1965) – with Stephen Spender's Introduction;
Signet paperback (New York, 1965);
Cape (London, 1967) – with Stephen Spender's Introduction;
Penguin (Harmondsworth, 1985) – with Lowry's correspondence with Cape.

BOOKS

Chris Ackerly & Lawrence J. Clipper, *A Companion to 'Under the Volcano'* (Vancouver, 1984).
Ronald Binns, *Malcolm Lowry* (London, 1984).
Gordon Bowker (ed.), *Malcolm Lowry Remembered* (London, 1985).
M. C. Bradbrook, *Malcolm Lowry: His Art and Early Life* (London, 1974).
Richard Hauer Costa, *Malcolm Lowry* (New York, 1972).
Douglas Day, *Malcolm Lowry: A Biography* (New York, 1973; London, 1974).
David Markson, *Malcolm Lowry's 'Volcano': Myth, Symbol, Meaning* (New York, 1978).
George Woodcock (ed.), *Malcolm Lowry: The Man and His Work* (Vancouver, 1971).
Howard J. Woolmer, *Malcolm Lowry: A Bibliography* (Revere, Penn., 1983).

ARTICLES AND ESSAYS

Charles Baxter, 'The Escape from Irony: *Under the Volcano* and the Aesthetics of Arson', *Novel*, 10 (Winter, 1977), pp. 114–26.
Roger Bromley, 'The Boundaries of Commitment: God, Lover, Comrade – Malcolm Lowry's *Under the Volcano* as a Reading of the 1930s', in Francis Barker (ed.), *1936: The Sociology of Literature*, 1979), pp. 273–96.

Matthew Corrigan, 'Malcolm Lowry, New York Publishing and the "New Illiteracy"', *Encounter*, 35 (July, 1970), pp. 82–93.

William H. Gass, 'In Terms of the Toenail: Fiction and the Figures of Life', in *Fiction and the Figures of Life* (New York, 1971) pp. 55–76; also printed in *New American Review*, 10 (1970).

Thomas B. Gilmore, 'The Place of Hallucination in *Under the Volcano*', *Contemporary Literature*, 23 (Summer, 1982) pp. 285–305.

Thomas York, 'The Post-Mortem Point of View in Malcolm Lowry's *Under the Volcano*', *Canadian Literature*, 99 (Winter, 1983), pp. 35–46.

The Malcolm Lowry Review (formerly *The Malcolm Lowry Newsletter*) is published twice a year by the Department of English, Wilfrid Laurier University, Ontario, Canada.

NOTES ON CONTRIBUTORS

WALTER ALLEN: critic and novelist; Professor of English, University of Ulster (1967–73); his novels include *Innocence is Drowned* (1938), *Rogue Elephant* (1946) and *Dead Men Over All* (1950); among his critical writings are *The English Novel: A Short Critical History* (1954), *Six Great Novelists* (1955) and *Tradition and Dream* (1964).

JACQUES BARZUN: American scholar and critic; Professor Emeritus of History, Columbia University, and Extraordinary Fellow of Churchill College, Cambridge; (1959), *Classic, Romantic and Modern* (1961), *The Use and Abuse of Art* (1974) and the edited volume of *Selected Letters of Lord Byron* (1953, 1957).

RONALD BINNS: author and critic; his publications include journal articles on Samuel Beckett, Mervyn Peak, John Fowles and J. G. Farrell, and the critical study, *Malcolm Lowry* (1984).

MALCOLM BRADBURY: critic, novelist and playwright; Professor of American Studies, University of East Anglia; his novels include *Eating People is Wrong* (1959), *The History Man* (1975) and *Rates of Exchange* (1983); among his works on literature are *What is a Novel?* (1969), *The Social Context of Modern English Literature* (1971), *Possibilities: Essays on the State of the Novel* (1973) and the Casebook on Forster's *A Passage to India* (1970).

RICHARD K. CROSS: Professor of English, University of California at Los Angeles; his publications include *Flaubert and Joyce: The Rite of Fiction* (1971) and *Malcolm Lowry: A Preface to His Fiction* (1980).

VICTOR DOYEN: Professor of English at the K.U.L. Catholic University at Leuven (Louvain) in Belgium.

DALE EDMONDS: Professor of English, Tulane University, New Orleans; among his publications are several studies of aspects of Lowry's work, and he is an editiorial consultant for the *Malcolm Lowry Newsletter*.

SHERRILL GRACE: Associate Professor of English, University of British Columbia; in addition to her work on Lowry, she has published articles on John Fowles and on the Canadian critic, Northrop Frye.

ROBERT B. HEILMAN: Professor Emeritus of English, University of Washington, Seattle, and editorial adviser to *Studies in the Novel, Modern Language Quarterly, Sewanee Review* and *Mississippi Studies in Literature*; his many publications include *English Drama Before Shakespeare* (1962), *Tragedy and*

Melodrama: Versions of Experience (1968), *The Ghost on the Ramparts and Other Essays in the Humanities* (1974), *The Ways of the World: Comedy and Society* (1978) and studies on Conrad, Hardy and Shakespeare.

BRIAN O'KILL: scholar and critic; Senior Lexicographer for the Longman Group of publishers, he has contributed to the *Longman Dictionary of the English Language* and several other dictionaries.

ANDREW J. POTTINGER: Canadian scholar; he has worked for several years on the original manuscripts held in the Lowry Collection at the University of British Columbia.

SIR STEPHEN SPENDER: poet, critic and editor; Professor of English, University College, London, 1968–73; a major figure in English letters since the 1930s, his *Collected Poems* were published in 1955, followed by further collections in 1971 and 1978; his studies in criticism include *The Destructive Element* (1935), *The Creative Element* (1954), *The Making of a Poem* (1955) and *The Thirties and After* (1978). He was knighted in 1983.

PHILIP TOYNBEE (1916–1981): critic, novelist and journalist; for many years principal reviewer for the *Observer*; his novels include *Tea with Mrs Goodman* (1947), *The Garden to the Sea* (1953) and *Views from a Lake* (1968) – the fourth novel in the 'Valediction of Pantaloon' sequence, begun in 1961. His *The Age of the Spirit: Religion as Experience* appeared in 1974.

BARRY WOOD: Professor of English, University of Houston, Texas; editor of *Malcolm Lowry: The Writer and His Critics* (1980).

JOHN WOODBURN: distinguished American book-reviewer; he died in 1948.

ACKNOWLEDGEMENTS

The author and publishers wish to thank the following for permission to use copyright material: Walter Allen, extract from review article, *New Statesman* (6 Sept. 1947), by permission of The Statesman & Nation Publishing Company Ltd; Ronald Binns, 'Materialism and Magic in *Under the Volcano*', *Critical Quarterly*, 23, No. 1 (1981), by permission of Manchester University Press; Malcolm Bradbury, 'Malcolm Lowry as Modernist' from *Possibilities: Essays on the State of the Novel* (1973), by permission of Oxford University Press. Copyright © by Malcolm Bradbury (1973); Richard K. Cross, extract from preface to *Malcolm Lowry: A Preface to His Fiction* (1980), by permission of The Athlone Press; Victor Doyen, 'Elements Towards a Spatial Reading of Malcolm Lowry's *Under the Volcano*', *English Studies*, 50 (1969), by permission of Swets Publishing Service; Dale Edmonds, '*Under the Volcano*: A Reading of the "Immediate Level"', *Tulane Studies in English*, 16 (1968), by permission of Tulane Studies in English; Sherrill Grace, extract from *The Voyage that Never Ends: Malcolm Lowry's Fiction* (1982), by permission of the University of British Columbia Press. Copyright © 1982 by the University of British Columbia Press; Robert B. Heilman, extract from review, *Sewanee Review*, LV, 3 (summer 1947), by permission of the editor of the *Sewanee Review*. Copyright © 1947, 1974 by the University of the South; Malcolm Lowry, preface to the French edition of *Under the Volcano*, translated by George Woodcock in his book *Malcolm Lowry: The Man and his Work* (1971), University of British Columbia Press, by permission of Literistic Ltd. Copyright © 1971 by the Estate of Malcolm Lowry; Brian O'Kill, 'Aspects of Language in *Under the Volcano*' from *The Art of Malcolm Lowry*, ed. Annie Smith (1978), Vision Press, by permission of the author; Stephen Spender, extract from preface to *Under the Volcano* (1967), by permission of Jonathan Cape Ltd and the Executors of the Malcolm Lowry Estate: Philip Toynbee, review 'Another Season in Hell', *The Observer* (29 April 1962), by permission of The Observer; Barry Wood, extract from the introduction to *Malcolm Lowry: Under the Volcano*, ed. Barry Wood (1980), by permission of Borealis Press Ltd.

Every effort has been made to trace all the copyright holders but if any have been inadvertently overlooked the publishers will be pleased to make the necessary arrangement at the first opportunity.

INDEX

Page numbers in **bold type** denote essays or extracts in this casebook. Names in SMALL CAPS are Lowry characters.